KNOW WHEN TO RUN

Lessons from the diary of a Gen X mom

Trisha L. Shepherd

DEDICATED TO

Ian, Calvin, Clara and Daisy May; our beloved families; and our friends who might as well be family. Thank you all for loving, forgiving and believing in me.

CONTENTS

Foreword ix

1. The Beginning of the End 1
2. The News Lady Wears Skulls 4
3. Final Countdown 7
4. Blistering Back into the Saddle 10
5. Ode to Sleep 12
6. Dishrag Mama and Chalk Milkshakes 14
7. Breast milk, Pinstripes and Funnel Clouds 16
8. Japanda 19
9. Don't F#%* with me 21
10. Motherworry 23
11. Four-decade Fiesta 25
12. Scared 28
13. A Horse Named Dan 30
14. Wonder Woman 32
15. Disposable Us 34
16. Groundhog Day 36
17. "This is depleting you" 38
18. "I don't want to do this anymore." 40
19. Spine of Steel 42
20. "But, you ordered it!" 44
21. Parenting Trick Ripped from the Headlines 47

22. Billboard-sized Insecurity · 50
23. A Midwife's Best Lesson · 52
24. Long Live Romance · 54
25. One Thing I'm Doing Right · 56
26. Nothing Compares · 58
27. Inhaling Apples · 61
28. "Everything is more beautiful with tequila." · 63
29. Angry Princess · 66
30. MetOl Fist (New Band. Theay Rock.) · 69
31. Fight or Flight? · 71
32. Thanksgiving Feast: 11:30 a.m. · 73
33. Rattling Chains · 75
34. "Out of My Cold, Dead Hands" · 78
35. Musical Medicine · 81
36. No Spurs Allowed · 83
37. Change of Power · 85
38. Knife in the Heart · 87
39. A Good Day · 89
40. Amish Spring Break · 91
41. The Aching Return of Dishrag Mama · 96
42. Viva, Las Vegas! · 98
43. Pseudo Single-Parenting · 102
44. A Seat in the Boys' Club · 104
45. "Me-time" Mishap · 107
46. Steps · 109
47. Cornfield Wedding · 111
48. Fairy Godmother · 113
49. When to Fold 'Em · 115
50. Over the Rainbow? · 118
51. The Message · 120
52. False Empty Nest · 122
53. The Offer · 124
54. Battle · 127

55. Free   129
56. Prost! (To the new chapter)   131
57. In the Wings   133
  Acknowledgements   135
  About Trisha Shepherd   139

FOREWORD

*L*istening. It's the hardest thing and the easiest thing to do. And when your life is in chaos, it's hard to hear even the clearest, loudest voices shouting to you: "Run! Get out of here! It is time to go!" The voices get lost in the mess of noise. Even if you do hear them, you try to deny them, because what they are telling you to do is scary.

I felt trapped in a fast-paced broadcasting career that had transitioned from exciting to all-consuming. I had landed a coveted position as a main news anchor in a big city, but the career that once brought me joy and fulfillment was starting to eat me alive. Every night, I carried with me onto that news desk a deep ache for more time with my children. I came very close to letting my job stop me from having a third child that my heart desperately wanted.

Voices all around me were whispering, nudging and finally shoving me in a new direction. But it took me a long, long time to hear them and believe them. Unlike the gambler in that Kenny Rogers song that my dad played so often when I was a kid, I didn't know when to walk away or know when to run.

I made a decision. I would write something every single day as I coped with my sadness, stress and confusion.

That one-year diary is like a video camera left rolling as a funnel cloud tore through. I had no idea when I began writing what a life-changing year I was about to document.

I wrote about dark (and sometimes shocking) twists and turns my life and career took. I also wrote about the joyful escapes that my wild, funny circle of friends provided—escapes that I now know were lifelines. They kept my spirit intact when that twister touched down.

Now, looking back at my own words, I can see a truth that was hidden to me then: my life would remain stuck in this storm until I listened to the wise voices coming at me from so many directions; my tornado sirens.

By the end of one dramatic year, I learned to listen. Then, it happened. A door opened to a whole new life.

My great hope is that someone else who is struggling with the 'too-muchness' of their life and career will see something familiar in my story and begin to listen their way into a better life.

CHAPTER 1

THE BEGINNING OF THE END

June 30

Well, today could have gone better. My agent called with the news: the television station's management is insisting on a brutal pay cut. Deep and ugly. If I want to keep my job anchoring the evening news in Indianapolis, I have to take it or leave it—and could I please let them know by Friday? Recession, budget cuts, market research—the list of "reasons" hardly mattered. It was a low ball offer, and it hurt. "I know, hon," my agent Sue said quietly. "It's not what we wanted. But they're not budging."

While I was talking anxiously on the phone, pacing the deck and picking up sticks from our neglected lawn, I could hear little Daisy May from the window above, wailing her lungs out. She is 6 weeks old and she was hungry. My new baby needed me and there I was, tied up on the phone working out a deal far crappier than I ever anticipated with the employer who would soon take me away from her nearly 10 hours per day.

I knew that having a baby so close to the end of my contract was a crazy gamble. TV news is a volatile business, and it's uglier than it has ever been. The business today is wildly different from the way it was when I began 14 years ago as a producer and reporter in Champaign, Ill. I climbed my way up to the anchor desk, got married and had our first baby. Things at work went south after a station buyout, and my husband Ian and I moved to Des Moines, Iowa for a bigger news gig. After our second child was born, we started targeting Indianapolis as our next, and hopefully final, move. (We liked Indy's easy-to-maneuver size, its promising career opportunities, and its proximity to my family in Chicago.)

When I was offered the main evening anchor job at an Indianapolis affiliate station, I felt like I had landed my "dream job." But three years and several management shifts later, with budgets cut to the bone and our ratings still lukewarm, my position was very much in jeopardy.

Along with all that job uncertainty, I had convinced myself we were just too insanely busy to add Baby #3 to the family. We already had two children, and between Ian's work as a musician and my evening news assignment, we were caught in an impossible scheduling scenario. But still, I could not stop thinking about teeny toes, baby powder and soft cotton onesies.

I had talked myself out of the baby business until our ninth wedding anniversary last spring. I almost fell out of my chair at the restaurant when Ian made the case for another child. He had noticed how mushy I got while holding our friends' newborn son. "If you want something badly enough, you make it work," he said, almost casually. "When does it ever make sense to have a kid anyway?" Wow, do I love this man—tattoos, drums and all.

So I found myself at age 35 looking forward to a May 15 due date and an August 27 end to my contract. And here I am now, smack in the middle. Staring at a sweet little sleeping face next to me on the couch; knowing that this is all that matters.

And knowing I am more determined than ever to find a job that feels worthy of the sacrifice of leaving my kids for so many precious hours each day.

LESSON: Moments of adversity reveal clarity. Listen to the urgent needs your heart reveals.

CHAPTER 2
THE NEWS LADY WEARS SKULLS

July 3

God Bless AMERICA, I am fried. It's 11:10 p.m. and I think we finally have all three kids asleep. Ian and I spent the evening with our kids and some friends in downtown Indy at an Indians (Minor League) ballgame, followed by fireworks in putrid heat and humidity.

The lowlight of the night was Daisy screaming the whole way home in traffic, and the scene of exhausted NEEDINESS that followed when we got home. Let's see if I can list the demands of our children:

Four-year-old Clara: "Find my other blankie! Carry me upstairs! Help me get my PJ's on! Brush my teeth! Take out my ponytail! Bring me some water with cold ice!" (The delicious redundancy of this phrase has not yet occurred to her.) "Close the shades, turn on the nightlight, and turn on my princess CD! And someone snuggle me! I am not USED to hearing fireworks in my bed."

Seven-year-old Calvin: "I want a piggyback ride up the stairs!" (Ian the Super Dad obliged, in spite of his wrecked back which has been through two recent surgeries.) "Help me make my bunk bed!" (He had stripped it for fun earlier in the day.) "And I need some ice water."

One-month-old Daisy: "Waaaaaahhhh!!" (Our baby only needed three things: a clean diaper, a fresh onesie and my boobs.)

I found myself holding a baby to my breast with one arm while using the other to throw sheets and a blanket on Cal's bed, take out Clara's ponytail and fill up water cups. Somewhere in the midst of this came some snippy moments between Ian and I about whether we should give in to the kids' demands, or simply tell them: JUST - GO - TO - BED!!!

I think maybe last night was payback for having too much fun over the last couple of days. My maternity leave is almost over, so yesterday I gave myself a legitimate "me-time" break with a girls' outing. I went to—oh hell, I almost can't stand to see this in writing—I went to see the latest teenage vampire romance flick. I know it is juvenile, ridiculous stuff, and I blame it all on my friend Andrea, who in turn blames it on me. It makes me feel better that she's a serious, intellectual person—a highly responsible professional woman and a mother of three—yet she's not ashamed to step up to the cashier and say, "One for 'Eclipse,' please." We both need breaks from our intense work and parenting realities. Immersing ourselves in the obsessive lust and drama of this cheesy vampire world seems to work.

As I slunk up to the ticket counter it occurred to me that my nerdiness was only enhanced by my new T-shirt. It is turquoise with very short sleeves, and a SKULL subtly peeking out from within a black floral pattern.

I swear I did not notice the skull when I bought the shirt. I had glanced at the shirt's color, the floral pattern, the price, and very importantly at this moment, the size—large enough to accommodate my impressive nursing mom chest. Done! It wasn't until after I got home that I noticed the shadowy skull cleverly hiding among the flowers.

I decided the shirt was way too funny to return. My inner bad-ass must have needed an outlet. I am wearing my skull shirt with gusto and hoping to leave people wondering what else they don't know about this "girl-next-door" news lady with the blonde bob.

Later in the afternoon, Ian and I took the kids for an Independence Day cookout with our friends Dean and Adrianna. Dean is one of Ian's old college buddies and closest friends, and it's easy to see why. He is a band geek-turned-successful-orchestra conductor with humor oozing out of every charismatic pore. "I got a bunch of fireworks—let's be all white trash!" Dean announced when we arrived at his house. We ate burgers off the grill, tipped back some beers, blew up cheap firecrackers and let our kids be kids. We toasted our bizarre Indiana laws, which make it a crime to buy booze on a Sunday, but allow stores to sell explosives that could take off your hand *right there in the grocery store next to the frozen pizzas,* any day of the week.

We updated our dear friends about my troubling contract situation at work, and even borrowed their printer to print out the foul document for me to sign. "F*&% them," Dean offered. He poured us another drink.

That's what friends are for.

LESSON: Friends and laughter are not frivolous. They are your lifelines. When things get dark, find them.

CHAPTER 3
FINAL COUNTDOWN

July 12

I am drenched in a quiet and melancholy mood today. Tomorrow I go back to work.

I have the house all to myself with little Daisy May. I'm trying half-heartedly to get the house in order before the full blast of my busy work life kicks in. I'd rather just lie on the floor, stare into those dreamy little brown eyes and talk to her about nothing. She is 8 weeks old.

By this time tomorrow, I'll be wearing a face full of makeup, my best red suit and high heels. I'll be staring at Daisy's picture on my desk and trying to put on a brave smile as I catch up with co-workers and tell them about life with my new daughter: "Yes, everything's going great! She's a wonderful baby, Cal and Clara are crazy about her, etc." I know what to say at first. But I'm still plotting my answer to the inevitable question, "So, are you ready to be back?"

I'm afraid to share the honest answer with people at work: HELL NO! Daisy has been fussier than normal, wanting to nurse all the time and sleeping very little between feedings. I think she is doing this just to make me even more hysterical about leaving her.

My boss called a few days ago to fill me in on my schedule when I return. Unfortunately, station management wants me to return to the 7 p.m. newscast, along with the 6 p.m. and 11 p.m. shows. The 7 p.m. duties will push my dinner/nursing break an hour later than I thought. Great.

I also found out that my co-anchor, Todd, has not been offered a new contract. Just a few years ago, our faces were all over billboards and buses as the station launched a huge publicity blitz to introduce viewers to the new "Todd and Trisha" anchor team. We've become partners in crime and true friends. Knowing that I'll have to go on without him sharing that anchor desk is a kick in the gut.

In spite of all this—AND the ugly pay cut from my recent contract negotiations—I found my inner people-pleasing, straight-A student shining through during the phone call. "Can't wait to get back in there!" I heard myself telling my news director. "Yes, things have been going great here at home but I feel ready to come back. Looking forward to Monday!" Why the hell did I have to sound so chipper and make it so easy on him? Sometimes I really disappoint myself.

Part of me really is ready to get back to the challenge of work and the camaraderie with my fun and talented co-workers. I just wish I could stop fantasizing about a part-time schedule. That kind of arrangement rarely exists in the world of TV news, where long, intense days, ferocious competition and unrelenting deadlines create a pressure-cooker work culture. In a perfect world I'd love to return to work maybe six months from now, on a part-time basis, and with flexibility to run home if a kid spikes a fever or the nanny calls in sick.

I'd also love a cook, a full-time housekeeper, a big savings account, kids who never argue with each other, a ballet dancer's body and hair that cooperates in humidity. They are all lovely fantasies, but nothing more than that. My life and career demand that I work full-time right now, and the best I can do is try my best to fit the puzzle pieces of work and family together without leaving gaping cracks.

I'm also realizing how stupid I would be not to stop and smell the roses. Every mother I know is crazy about her kids, even if they stress her out sometimes. But I'm realizing that lots of women are not all that crazy about their men. Ian and I aren't immune to marital tension, but overall, after nine years of marriage, we are still very, very close. Somehow the passion and attraction have not faded under the strain of having three kids (in three different states, nonetheless!) and unrelenting, weird work schedules.

Our dear friend Mindy claims that on the night she introduced us, "the rest of the room stood still, and sparks FLEW!" (As a thespian, and the world's-best kindergarten teacher, she has quite a flair for the dramatic, but I have to pretty much agree.) Ian was gone all last week, and when he got home late last night there was so much emotion in his embrace as I wrapped myself in his arms. I can't wait to spend some time with him this evening. We've been able to draw closer by giving each other so much independent time and space.

We may look like an unlikely pair—the tattooed musician and the girl-next-door news lady—but I can't imagine my life with anyone else. I have a rock of support to lean on. I have a shoulder to cry on.

And I may need them both like never before tomorrow.

Lesson: Telling yourself to "smell the roses" when you are miserable means you are in denial of your genuine emotions. Don't dismiss the fantasies that dominate your imagination, or the weight that pushes your shoulders down. Listen to the inner voice of heart when it screams at you.

CHAPTER 4

BLISTERING BACK INTO THE SADDLE

July 13

It's day one back in the saddle on the news desk. I have blisters from the pretty new patent leather heels I bought to try to make myself feel pulled-together and professional after eight weeks in flip flops and baggy t-shirts. It's strange seeing real makeup on my face again. Luckily for me, Daisy was sound asleep when it was time for me to leave. No tears for me—at least not until later.

I was holding it together just fine, until a co-worker (who is also a mom) asked me with genuine concern how I was doing. DANGIT. There went my composure.

I stopped myself from telling her the whole truth as my eyes filled with tears I could no longer hide. The truth? I HATED everything about leaving that child. Dreaded this day. Hated coming back to the long, draining hours. Couldn't stop worrying. Couldn't wait to have that baby back in my arms.

But that's not the story people want to hear. (At least, I assume they don't.) So I found myself choking back the tears and giving her the standard answer: "She's doing great, kids are doing great, everything's great, great, great! Yep, it's a little hard leaving her, but she's in great hands, did I mention we're all doing GREAT?"

As my friend Andrea pointed out in a back-to-work pep talk, it's a gift to show my children "the importance of doing something with your life that is meaningful, and about which you are passionate."

I totally agree. I'm just not sure this path exactly qualifies.

Lesson: Be thankful for those in your life who allow you to be real; those who you can trust to love the unedited version of you.

CHAPTER 5
ODE TO SLEEP

July 15

I'm starting to get used to that dizzy feeling—the one that keeps a tiny little voice in my mind begging at the most inappropriate times, "Just lay that head down for five minutes, I promise it'll be worth it!"

I was fully prepared for this, having been through it twice before, and am quite proud of the way I can suck it up and deal with the exhaustion.

4 a.m. feeding? Hand me the remote and I'll infomercial my way through the yawns. 5 a.m. diaper change after I just got back to sleep? Let me gaze at that tiny face and I can shrug off that stinky interruption in a few skillful seconds.

What is starting to get me, though, is how SHALLOW the sleep is during those precious hours between interruptions. I am a soldier on patrol – sleeping with one eye open, waiting to spring into action.

Many of my friends confirm what I've noticed: this problem is way more pervasive for new moms than new dads. I am sometimes envious of Ian's drum-induced hearing loss. I wake up with every tiny sigh, grunt, and rustle from the bassinet. He can snore through a baby wailing or a screaming alarm clock RIGHT NEXT TO HIS HEAD. Many mornings he'll wake up and ask, "Wow, did she make it through the whole night?" That's when my red, swollen eyes narrow and lock with his, as I begin dreaming up some kind of shock device for his side of the bed that is triggered by a baby's cry.

That's not to say he's unwilling to help overnight. Ian all but begs me to wake him up and have him cover an overnight feeding so I can get more rest. I've let him do this a couple of times, but it's pointless. I lay there and listen to the entire feeding process, worrying. How stupid is that? "Sleep, dammit!!!" I scold myself. Then I'm worried and pissed off. And just as tired in the morning.

I keep reminding myself that very, very soon, I'll be worrying when she DOESN'T wake me up in the middle of the night; missing those little grunts and cries.

In the meantime, I'm leaning pretty hard on my afternoon cup of coffee to get my energy up for the evening newscasts, and my TV quality concealer to cover the dark circles under my eyes.

This sleepless stage won't last forever.

And even if it did, she'd be worth it.

Lesson: Your body doesn't lie. Pay attention when you are reaching your physical limits. Listen to your body. Stop the bleeding before you become drained.

CHAPTER 6
DISHRAG MAMA AND CHALK MILKSHAKES

July 16

It's finally Friday and I feel like a dishrag that's been wrung out thoroughly and left to dry on a forgotten clothesline; drained and empty with absolutely nothing left to give, beginning to get stiff and brittle as the last drops of moisture evaporate from me in slow motion. This is me: Dishrag Mama.

Today I volunteered to go out on a live shot for the 5 p.m. news, then returned and anchored the other three newscasts. I was out in the nasty heat and humidity, and the subject matter I was reporting on made it feel more oppressive. I was delivering live reports outside a house where seven people were murdered, including three children, recounting the hideous crime as the house was finally being demolished. The entire neighborhood has a sad, heavy feel, with lots of boarded-up windows, weeds and litter.

As I stood in front of the piles of brick and dirt where the house of horrors used to sit, I noticed strange music in the distance. It was off-key, a little slow and disjointed. A cell phone ringing? The eerie tune grew louder and I realized what it was: a makeshift ice cream truck, looking just as sad and run-down as the neighborhood, slinking down the block like a scene from a horror movie. I couldn't wait to leave.

As I raced back to the TV station to prepare for the other newscasts, I thought about how fortunate I felt to be able to drive away from that neighborhood; fortunate that no matter how exhausting it may be, I have a job that provides my family with a safe place to live.

After the newscasts I made my typical mad dash home to nurse a wailing, hungry, and impatient baby. My "dinner break" almost never involves sitting down to eat. It's a whirlwind of homework, nursing, baths and bedtime stories.

This evening as I pulled into the driveway I took note of the collection of junk my kids had left all over the yard: a boomerang; a wax gorilla; a miniature bunny wearing a dress; several baseball gloves and balls; a plastic tiger; a skateboard; a foam noodle; and our BLENDER filled with sidewalk chalk and water.

I guess someone had more fun on this fine summertime Friday than I did.

And I guess that's the whole point.

Lesson: Sometimes we are most open to truth when we are exhausted. When you are fragile, vulnerable and drained, open your eyes and ears to the lessons around you. Let your world affect your heart.

CHAPTER 7
BREAST MILK, PINSTRIPES AND FUNNEL CLOUDS

July 19

There's breast milk on my pinstripes and a funnel cloud over Trafalgar, Ind. I'm in the lounge just upstairs from the newsroom scrambling to fit a quick breast-pump break into a busy night of breaking news. In my rush, a piece of the pump slips out of my hand, spilling some of that liquid gold onto my best suit. Bloody hell! I call home to check in on hungry Daisy May who is barely tolerating a bottle. My mom just arrived to help me with the kids while Ian is working out of town, and I had really hoped to stop home on my dinner break to get her settled in and nurse that sweet baby. Damn this stormy Indiana weather. "Welcome to my life," I say.

So I'm left trying to hide the stain on my suit and keep my head in the game at work while my heart is aching for my baby girl. It's one more twist in an already very strange day. This afternoon I found myself sitting on the anchor desk with a guy named Todd, whom I'd met just 10 minutes earlier. He seems very nice, but it's an awkward situation. He is apparently about to replace my current co-anchor who, in an awkward twist of fate, is also named Todd. Old Todd and I had a field day with this. "At least they can re-use all the 'Todd and Trisha' paraphernalia they made for us, just cover me up with a new face," my soon-to-be-ex partner mused.

How quickly things change in this business. One day they're plastering your face on giant billboards, shipping you all over the state to meet mayors and shake hands at county fairs, and bombarding TV viewers with endless ads showcasing your experience, talent and charm. Two news directors and one expensive consultant later, they're introducing New Todd while Old Todd is tossed aside. I'm painfully aware of how fortunate I am supposed to feel to have kept my job, and how easily I might also have been thrown aside had I not just returned from maternity leave, when the Family and Medical Leave Act says it's not kosher to fire you. (Although apparently giving a new mom a huge "take it or leave it" pay cut is just fine. Hmmmm...)

On days like this, I can always use an extra dose of positive, calming energy from my colleague Kevin, the meteorologist. He has an incredible talent for keeping a clear head and a bright outlook during even the toughest situations (including tornado outbreaks, as is often the case in Indiana.) *I have never, not even once, heard him swear.* That is almost physically impossible when you work in a newsroom.

I've asked Kevin many times to let me in on his secrets for managing the difficult hours, the stress, and the uncertainty of the television business. "I figure I'm just riding a big wave," he's told me. "I just try not to let things get to me, and see how long I can keep staying upright." (This is why he is so adored by both co-workers and viewers!)

One of my co-workers has a magic 8 ball on her desk. Tonight before I left work, I shook it, and asked if this is the right business for me to stay in.

"It is certain," the ball answered.

But am I?

Lesson: Some days are the perfect storm of challenges. Hold on for dear life to anything that helps you find humor or comfort on those days, and know that this, too, shall pass.

CHAPTER 8
JAPANDA

July 20

I love that Clara studies geography at school. Every night as we tuck her in, we love each other past a new place. "I love you past Florida!" she'll say. "Well, I love you past Europe," I counter. Some nights she loves me past Texas, Italy and Infinity.

One night, she loved me past "Japanda." That one is hard to top.

But the other night I thought I had one-upped her to the ultimate degree. "I love you past the Universe," I told her. "And past Forever."

"I love you past HEAVEN. And EVERYTHING," she told me. Case closed.

I know that as years go by a lot of our memories will turn as mushy as her infamous sidewalk chalk in the blender, but I hope Ian and I will always remember how hilarious, sweet, strong-willed and how very unique our girl was when she was 4 years old.

I love her past Florida. Past Japanda. Past Forever. Past Heaven.

Lesson: Remember that no matter how dark your days may be, your children forgive you and love you. Soak in their love, all the way to heaven, Florida and Japanda.

CHAPTER 9
DON'T F#%* WITH ME

July 22

I have had a DAY. I'm in complete "don't f#%* with me" mode right now. I've been rushed since the moment I got up. I could no longer put off getting my out-of-control hair trimmed (occupational hazard: news anchors don't get much slack for bad hair days.) Fitting in a salon visit meant I had to get myself ready for work, buy a few groceries, extinguish a major Calvin and Clara fight, and nurse Daisy—twice—before 11:30 a.m.

I also got a message on my cell from my health insurance company, basically explaining that yes indeed, they have correctly handled the claim I've been inquiring about. They are covering a whopping $120 of my bill for Daisy's birth. After five phone calls, I still can't seem to make anyone understand that this was CHILDBIRTH, not a routine exam. I tried to explain to the insurance representative on the phone, "See, I went in to the birth center PREGNANT, and emerged with a squirmy and cute BABY." She failed to see any humor. Although I'm no medical billing expert, $120 hardly seems a "reasonable and customary" price for childbirth, but that's what their codes are insisting.

The night got further complicated when I was handed a late assignment: "14-year-old thwarts burglary attempt by locking himself in a bathroom with a phone—details at 11." I had to make my "dinner break" lightning quick because I had a report to put together. With my mom in town watching the kids, I really wanted to check in at home. I raced home and arrived to find Calvin and Clara in tears because they'd gotten in BIG STINKING TROUBLE for overall wildness, followed by unspeakable sassiness.

"Grandma is evil!" Clara told me loudly, within easy earshot of my frazzled mother. Adding to my horror, I discovered they had locked the master bathroom shut from the outside by clicking the button on the doorknob, stepping outside and slamming the door shut. They did it *just for fun,* so no one could get in.

I forced apologies out of my hellions, nursed baby Daisy until she was full and smiley, and raced out the door as my mom began trying to jimmy the bathroom door open with a credit card and screwdriver.

I could have used a different kind of screwdriver right about then.

When I got home late tonight, I headed upstairs, needing a fix. I stood quietly and stared at Daisy's sleeping face. One thought pounded through my exhausted head: "I am *so glad* we decided to have this child."

Everything worthwhile comes at a cost. She is so, so worth it.

Lesson: Mama said there'd be days like this. She was right. Everyone has them. Focus on the good. Things will get better.

CHAPTER 10
MOTHERWORRY

July 25

I stayed up a little too late last night having an overdue heart-to-heart with my mom. We've always had a good relationship, and she has showered me with love and support for as long as I can remember. But we tend to stay away from anything too deep or emotional. I *hate* letting my parents see me upset or even vulnerable. I guess I just don't want them worrying about me.

This conversation needed to happen, though. I needed my worried mother to know that as much as I appreciate her support and love for me, it would mean even more if I felt her love and support for *us*—Ian and me.

There's been a growing amount of tension between them, mainly because she usually visits when he's traveling for work. She sees how difficult it is for me to manage the house, kids and job on my own when he's gone. But she never gets to see the ordinary weekdays, when Ian is the most hands-on dad I know, taking care of every detail at home during my long work shifts. He works a lot of evenings and weekends but his schedule right now allows him to be home at least two days during the week to hold down the fort while I work from 2 p.m. until midnight.

I also know there's a stigma attached to being a musician. Everyone knows unless you're a major rock star the pay isn't outstanding and the hours are difficult. I'm sure my parents would feel more at ease if he had a more conventional job that meant a more conventional schedule, along with higher pay and benefits to take the pressure off me. Sometimes, I'll admit, I think about that too. But, I reminded my mom, that's not who he is, and I knew that from the moment I met him. Music is more than his hobby. It's an all-consuming passion. It's a part of his soul and it's what keeps him alive. I love him wholeheartedly, not *in spite of* that passion, but in large part *because of it*. And he loves me in a complete, unblinking, wonderful way.

I also pointed out that the difficulty of our daily routine is just as much a result of *my* crazy nighttime work hours as it is his work. He's a much better spouse and father than my parents will ever know, I tearfully told my mother.

"If you're truly happy, then that's all I need to know," she assured me. "I just don't want you to make the mistake I made when you kids were growing up, and be afraid to speak up and ask for help when I needed it. You need to have a voice."

She has a point. I *hate* asking for help. Even when it's offered, I sometimes hesitate to accept it. I need to get better at that. Someday I'm sure I will worry about my own kids, eyeing their spouses suspiciously if there seems to be any kind of struggle in their lives. I can imagine how hard it would be for me to watch my own kids as adults slugging their way through days as exhausting as mine tend to be.

I really hope my parents and Ian and I can all find a little more harmony. This talk wasn't easy, but it felt like a pretty good first step.

Lesson: When something in your relationship with a loved one is bothering you, speak up. Be brave. Be honest. Don't hide your struggles. They will still love you.

CHAPTER 11
FOUR-DECADE FIESTA

July 30

To mow or not to mow.

Today is Ian's 40th birthday, and earlier today, while he was at work, I was getting ready to host a party. The OCD part of me wanted the house spotless and the lawn looking great. The realist in me knew this was about as likely as being struck by lightning and winning the lottery. Twice. And the wannabe attachment-parenting-baby-wearing-touchy-feely-mama in me said, "Spend that precious time on the children instead! Hire someone to do the dirty work or just let it go."

My neighbor-friend Jill—an energetic pilates instructor and runner with mile-a-minute energy and humor—gave me the phone number for a neighborhood lawn boy. I called. He was out of town. "Well, just stick a bow on Daisy's head and call her your excuse!" Jill told me.

Really, between working full time, nursing a newborn and parenting two kids on summer break from school, I have plenty of excuses not to have a house that looks like a magazine picture. These are some of our nearest and dearest friends, who would never, ever, even for a second, judge our dust and overgrown grass.

Why did I even care then? Why? Why? *Why?*

So, of course I found myself racing against the clock, the baby, and the impending rain to get that stupid lawn cut. I stuck Clara on baby duty, asking her to push Daisy up and down the driveway in the stroller while I flew up and down the big front lawn. I had to stop once to end a fight between Cal and Clara, and about three times to pacify Daisy. The crooked stripes on the lawn suggest I must have been sipping martinis beforehand, but I promise I was not drunk, just horribly distracted. I finished, triumphant, just as big, fat raindrops began to fall and Daisy started to lose it completely. Mission accomplished.

Ian's 40th turned out to be a magical, memorable occasion. Barbecue, booze, and babysitters for the kids were a magic combination. Although Ian is a musician, he doesn't usually like the spotlight, preferring to hide out behind the drum set. I know he was a little nervous about a whole event focusing on him. But once we got a little bit (well, a lot) of whiskey in him, he was the life of the party, totally humbled by the outpouring of affection.

His nearest and dearest friend, Scott, traveled all the way from L.A. for the occasion. Scott and I have always gravitated toward each other because his relationship with his artsy wife has so many parallels with my relationship with my musician husband. We both work in media careers. We both work too hard, and we both are likely to blow up under our own self-inflicted pressure if we don't blow off steam sometimes. Scott works for NPR, and is in charge of getting huge corporate sponsors to cough up incredible sums of money, or something to that effect. He must do it well because in just a few years they've promoted him and moved him from Chicago, to L.A., and he's about to move up again, to New York. Sometimes when I'm around Scott, I feel like giving him incredible sums of money too (if only I had any). He is that cool and charismatic. But, most importantly, he is a loyal and longtime friend to Ian and to me.

After several strong cocktails, Scott and I found ourselves plotting an entrepreneurial move: "I'll be the money-getter, you be the talent. This could be awesome!" he proposed. He says he thinks I should be doing something bigger than local commercial TV news, and is eager to see me dive into something more redeeming. "Come to the light – come to NPR!" He kept pushing: "We just have to find the exact right format—the right gig!"

It sounds so appealing. I would love to work in an environment a little less soul-sucking, and a little more organic, artistic, forward-thinking, insightful. Could Scott be the key to helping me make that leap? My gears are spinning…

Lesson: Treasure the friends who stick with you through thick and thin. Listen to their cheerleading. Believe what they think you are capable of.

CHAPTER 12
SCARED

August 2

I 've shed lots of tears today. I am more than a little scared about what's suddenly going on with Ian. Today he was more impatient and agitated than I have seen him in years. His nerves seemed absolutely fried under the weight of a long string of backbreaking days with the kids.

Cal and Clara have been really tough to deal with during these long summer days. They are bored and up in each other's business. *School cannot start soon enough.*

But tonight, it went from bad to worse. After I returned to work from my dinner break, Daisy apparently added fuel to the fire by screaming for two hours straight. It was the perfect storm.

I came home to a wailing, red-faced, sweaty baby and a fried husband. He was pacing, muttering to himself, and telling me, "All that baby does is f-ing scream! You have no idea! All you have to do is stick a boob in her face and she's happy. I get a screaming baby, every time! I can't….take this…any….more."

It was an honest and well-earned moment of frustration, but one that didn't exactly help ease my gut-wrenching sadness about having to work so many hours. Ian is absolutely right that the whole breastfeeding deal gives moms an unfair advantage over dads. I don't blame Daisy for spitting out the bottle and screaming for the real thing. The only problem is I'm sitting on a news desk several miles away at the very time she's screaming for Mama's milk.

What's killing me is this: it's hard enough for me to go to work when I know everything's *great* at home. It's damned near impossible to keep myself together when I know things are bordering on apocalyptic in my house.

I hate that I can't see a solution. Ian and I have never known the luxury of having parents in town to relieve us when we hit our breaking point or get into a desperate child care bind. In each place we've lived, we've had to build up our own village of friends and babysitters. I can't bring myself to ask our friends for more favors right now, and we certainly can't afford to hire more help from sitters.

I worry about Cal and Clara and how they pick up on all this unrest, anxiety and resentment. I worry about Daisy, screaming for hours inconsolably. I worry about Ian, drowning in stress, then racked with guilt.

And I worry about myself. How can I keep this ship from sinking? How can I make everyone in this family okay and happy and still keep my job? I don't even have the energy to care about what makes *me* happy. It's all spent on maintaining everyone else's well-being. The ONLY thing I want is for everyone in my household to be okay.

I have some serious praying to do tonight.

Lesson: We all have breaking points. Don't be afraid to pull the brakes when you or your partner hit a wall.

CHAPTER 13

A HORSE NAMED DAN

August 4

I took Calvin on his first horseback ride today. Things have been hard for all of us. He's been bummed out lately that summer is almost over, and I wanted to distract him with an adventure in the great outdoors.

The cowgirl in charge at the saddle barn assigned him to ride "Dan," a brown and white spotted horse with a geriatric charm. Dan's pace of about one mile-per-hour was perfect for a nervous first-time cowboy. After just a few minutes, Cal started to relax in his saddle. He began to chatter nonstop as we headed deep into the tranquil woods of the state park. His voice was nearly drowned out by the roar of locusts.

I breathed in the smell of the wood and dirt and leaves and creek water, stared up at those trees as tall as skyscrapers, and realized I could not stop smiling. I was free from deadlines and worries. I stared at the long rays of sunlight streaming from between the endless, towering tree trunks. I took a snapshot in my mind.

I want to hold onto this memory with my boy: our turbulent moods dissolving in the cool air of an ancient forest, disappearing step by step to the slow, steady gait of a horse named Dan.

Lesson: When tension gets high, go into the woods to get out of your head.

CHAPTER 14

WONDER WOMAN

August 5

I am Wonder Woman today. I muscled our trio through the grocery store this morning with Daisy in the Baby Bjorn, Clara "driving" the giant cart with a car on the front and Calvin pushing his own mini-cart. I wanted a strong sedative by the time we got done, but at least I managed to remember the most critical item on the list: diapers.

I got the dishes done, laundry started, myself showered and baby nursed, kids lunched. Then I headed in for a grueling day at work. Before I even got on the interstate I got a phone call from the newsroom. "There's been a mass shooting today. Get ready to hustle."

I got sent out to a rough neighborhood in sauna-like heat to cover an emotional gathering of grieving family members and enraged community leaders. I raced against the deadline to get my story into the 5 p.m. news, returned to the TV station and ran upstairs to pump Daisy some milk for tomorrow, anchored the newscasts at 6 and 7, then stayed late to shoot a bunch of fancy promos with New Todd telling viewers to watch us. I ate a burrito in the car as I jetted home for my late "dinner break," nursed crying Daisy until she was happy again, read Clara a book about Barbie and read Cal a book about poisonous snakes. I left them with the sitter and hurried back to the station, put together a new story on the shooting victims for the 11 p.m. news and checked in with my stressed-out hubby by phone as he drove home from his own wild day at work. I rallied every last drop of energy left to prop myself up on the anchor desk for one last show.

I am daydreaming right now that I will go to bed tonight and magically wake up in a cabin in the mountains—a cool, crisp morning with a field of wildflowers and a creek bubbling over rocks right next to my window (my favorite sound in the world). No clocks, no responsibilities. I sit on the porch, sip my coffee slowly, stare at the flowers and the water and the sky, and breathe.

And then, I turn my head and look at the handsome guy sitting next to me. I grab his hand, put my head on his shoulder, and just sit. Together. Peaceful. Whole. Free.

Lesson: When things get tough, you may find yourself tempted to overcompensate by trying to be a superhero. Listen to the fantasies that pull you toward a quieter, more serene version of yourself.

CHAPTER 15
DISPOSABLE US

August 7

Last night we threw a little bon voyage party for my outgoing co-anchor, Todd. It was the first time I'd seen him unshaven. He looked great. Relaxed. A little stubble doesn't matter when you're not putting your mug on TV every night. He and his wife Valarie seem to be taking it all incredibly well. Part of me wishes he were staying, another part is incredibly envious that he moving on to an inevitably greener pasture.

It doesn't make sense. This business treats us as though we are disposable. My former partner is committed, hard-working and talented. And it doesn't matter.

The only thing I can think to do now is to continue kicking ass at work and at home, trying to keep myself employed so I can keep feeding my kids.

I am working on my internal pep talks and pushing myself at work. It's time for me to start showing off what kind of journalist I am—not to impress my managers, but to convince myself that what I do 9+ hours a day is worth the sacrifice of leaving my kids.

Lesson: Don't let a dog-eat-dog industry shake your confidence in your abilities. When hard work and talent aren't rewarded in your workplace, search for a new place where they are.

CHAPTER 16

GROUNDHOG DAY

August 12

Last night I re-discovered a video diary I put together three-and-a-half years ago. It was part of a project I launched for my TV station at the time, documenting the challenges facing Generation X moms (a topic just a LITTLE bit close to my heart). I was an early morning news anchor at the time, and to create this video diary I carried a camera throughout my entire insane day (which began at 2:30 a.m.) to examine my work-life "balance." HA!

Looking back at that snapshot of my life frozen in time, three things jumped out at me: I looked a LOT younger then. Seriously, the last three years aged me at least 10 years.

Three years later, it's the *same story*, different setting. It's freaking Groundhog Day.

I actually said out loud in that video, "If I could just find a way to get a little more time to myself, and little more time with my husband, and a little more sleep, then it would all be great."

YES. Bingo, baby! Only that was *impossible* while working those hours.

I was getting up at 2:30 every morning, working a 7-8 hour day, then taking over duty with kids until climbing into bed at 8:30, just as Ian arrived home from work. The look of exhaustion on my face and body at the end of the day still kind of stuns me. I remember it, sort of, but it's all a big fog.

Now, it's the same problem in reverse. I wake up early, parent all morning, rush off to work the rest of the night, and get to bed very late. There is still no "me" time to speak of, not enough couple time and *never* enough sleep.

I still feel lucky to have a good job in a field I love. I know I'm making the most of my hours at home with the kids. I think at this point in my life, though, I am a little more concerned about all that gets shoved aside when every waking moment I have is about kids or work. It's time to figure out how to sneak more R&R into the schedule somehow before I burn out completely and turn to dust.

But how? When? Three years later, I am still waiting to figure that out.

Lesson: Listen to your past to find a path to a better present. When difficult patterns in your life are stuck on repeat, don't just lift the needle. Play a different record.

CHAPTER 17
"THIS IS DEPLETING YOU"

August 14

It was about midnight in our kitchen. "So I've been thinking," said Ian's always thought-provoking stepdad, Paul, as he poured himself some Gentleman Jack Whiskey with a slice of fresh lime. "Maybe it's time you got into a different profession."

Plenty of my friends have suggested as much when they've seen me struggle with the difficult schedule and even more difficult managers over the course of my career in local TV news. But when Paul says it, there's a certain gravitas that makes me sit up and take notice.

His voice has always reminded me a bit of Garrison Keilor, the host of *A Prairie Home Companion* on NPR. Both men share an educated, polished, deliberate manner of speech, but Paul likes to insert an occasional—and perfectly enunciated— expletive for emphasis. He's a former physician and public health director, and although he's lived in the U.S. for more than 20 years he maintains a very Canadian sensibility and accent. Maybe it's the voice, maybe it's the education, maybe it's the gray beard, but I find his wisdom awfully hard to ignore.

"It seems to me you're wasting your talent on this business that's really starting to head down the toilet," Paul told me. "You have so much to offer. I can see how much this is depleting you."

It seems like every time Paul and Susan (Ian's mom) come to visit, they catch our family in the height of chaos, and this week was no exception. With Ian working dawn till dusk at the Drum Corps International championships, me getting dealt the State Fair assignment, Daisy still not quite sleeping through the night, and the two older kids still at home for the summer, there was no possible way we could keep up. Paul made a grocery run when he found our fridge void of milk, juice, or anything edible for lunch. "A mission of mercy!" he declared. He returned with—I'm not kidding—SEVEN boxes of cereal, along with all the missing staples PLUS some fresh fruits and veggies he found at a roadside stand. It was beyond embarrassing. But much-appreciated.

At any rate, the combination of personal and professional stress has kick-started my soul-searching once again. What could I do that would be as fulfilling, creative, and interesting, minus the crazy hours, instability, and ugly office politics? How do I find it? Will I know it when I see it?

And when I get there, how hard will I kick myself for not making the jump sooner?

Lesson: Listen to your rocks of support. Their voices are helping you hear what you already know.

CHAPTER 18

"I DON'T WANT TO DO THIS ANYMORE."

August 29

I don't want to do this anymore.

I want to look back and remember August 29, 2010, as the day I finally declared out loud to myself and to my husband that I am officially breaking up with my career. It's about damned time.

It was a rough week at work, and I realized that nearly everything I have treasured and enjoyed about my work in TV news is being whittled away, sidelined, or upstaged by the parts I can't stand. It is no longer something I can feel good about. It just isn't "me." Not like it used to be.

The most redeeming part about being a TV journalist has been the occasional ability to tell a really profound, interesting and insightful story. Even though my anchor desk duties tend to make these stories kind of few and far between, until this point I've felt I had *just enough* to keep me fueled.

This week I brought a list of ideas for in-depth stories I'm interested in working on to our newsroom's managing editor. He's the guy who knows everything about everything (or thinks he does) and loves to tell you all about it, but tends to be literally asleep at the head of the table when you're pitching your own ideas.

His response to my contributions: Thanks, but no thanks. My ideas were of no interest to him. He'd rather see the main anchor working on the big "gets," interviewing the major players in the tragedy du jour; the juicy sort of train wreck interviews that are hard to take your eyes off and easy to promote in a 10-second spot. It's my least favorite type of reporting: sensational; exploitative; flash-in-the-pan; painful.

I told all of this to Ian tonight. It's a lot like deciding you're going to leave your spouse, but not having anywhere to go yet. I can't quite picture what I want to do next, but I just realized that that's okay. There are lots of possibilities out there. This is the step I had to make first. I'm clearing out that space in my brain that was holding out hope of finding a way to make this job work. Now, there's room for clearer answers to enter.

I am so *done* with spending my days and nights at a job that isn't fitting me. I am so *over* the anxiety and conflict I feel about it. So ready to hand in my two-weeks' notice and celebrate with Ian by downing a bottle of champagne. But I have to find my parachute first.

My prayer tonight is for my mind to be open enough to know it when I see it.

Lesson: Moments of clarity are earth-shattering, and fleeting. Don't let your fear of change dim their power.

CHAPTER 19

SPINE OF STEEL

September 15

The good news: today is payday. The bad news: it's the first pay-check under my "less is more" pay scale. In celebration, the universe has conspired to challenge our financial stability by offering us a broken toilet, a stalled car battery, a leaking sink and an internet/phone outage. As I write, there are two guys working on the cable and phone wires, two more guys dismantling our toilet and a pile of dirty dishes in the sink.

Since my moment of clarity a couple of weeks ago I feel I've really turned a corner. It feels good to be certain about what I DON'T want and know that an end to this maddening business climate and strangling schedule is coming. On Sunday night I sat down at the computer (with a huge glass of red wine and a bowl of potato chips) and completed an application, resume and cover letter for a children's hospital PR job.

Working on a couple of health-related stories lately made me realize how much I connect with people facing illnesses. Some of it is probably my natural bleeding-heart empathy for anyone suffering. But I suspect a lot of it also came from my adventures with scoliosis as a kid.

With my spine curved like an "s," I went through three years wearing an awkward back brace before going under the knife at age 13. One of my most vivid memories from my self-conscious and shy pre-adolescence is being asked to disrobe in front of a handful of young medical residents so they could line up and see what a *really* messed up spine looked like. (If that doesn't take a jack-hammer to a tween's self-esteem, I'm not sure what would.) Even so, my parents and I understood why this was important. It was a teaching hospital, and we knew that the next generation of doctors needed opportunities to see REAL patients with REAL conditions, even if that meant adding an extra layer of awkwardness to my exams.

The doc straightened my spine as much as he could, added steel Harrington rods and fused the vertebrae using bone chips harvested from my hip. It wasn't a fun experience, and I am left with a few battle wounds. I know what it feels like to be a terrified kid entering an OR with fears of never waking up. I know what it feels like to be stuck in a hospital unable to even sit up without help, fighting back tears of pain and fear. I know what it feels like to learn to walk all over again. My shoulders will always stay noticeably crooked. I have a thin, pale scar straight down the middle of my back, and a thicker one on my hip. I move a little bit like the Tin Man. While most days are fine, I've gotten used to working through days filled with pain.

I also have stainless steel rods in my back that will stay in place forever. Facing something that big when I was so young has literally left me with a spine of steel.

I have a feeling I'm going to need it very soon.

Lesson: Wounds that leave you feeling "damaged" give you your greatest strength. Own your struggles and use them to find both empathy and power.

CHAPTER 20

"BUT, YOU ORDERED IT!"

September 20

Well, that didn't take long. My little fling with becoming a hospital PR staffer has ended abruptly and fruitlessly. I found out the salary for the position I thought I wanted is less than half of my newly-reduced TV salary. Aside from selling the house, cars, or children, I can't see how we'd make that work. So I'm on to Plan B. At least, I'm searching for it.

I think I'm getting several very different issues confused: the grueling schedule of TV news, the less-than-savory twists the news business in general is taking, and the maddeningly unhealthy atmosphere in my current newsroom.

There are days when the schedule drives me up a tree, such as when Clara clings to me and BEGS me not to go back to work as I'm tucking her in to bed. That's when I get weak and start to fantasize about working any kind of "normal" 9 to 5, even if it means giving up the creative stuff I love.

"When will you have to work only in the daytime, Mom?" Clara asked me the other day. "You ORDERED it on the computer!" It took me a minute to realize that when she saw me filling out that job application online, she thought I was literally ordering up a new job with a better schedule. *"Click here to add to shopping cart."*

Even if it were that simple, what would I click? It's so tempting to just jump into something that seems safe and less demanding; to pour my heart into my children at the expense of my creative and professional drive. "So many people become zombies about the whole parenting thing," our friend Scott (the impossibly hip and ambitious NPR management guy) told me by phone from L.A. today. "They turn everything in their lives over to their kids and don't even stop to think about it. But that's just not us."

Scott thinks big. He loves his three kids and his wife madly, and he loves chasing his ambition. He doesn't torture himself the way I do about time he spends away. Why? First of all, I get the sense he enjoys his work way more than I enjoy mine. He works hard, but he has been consistently rewarded for his work, and he's in an internationally-respected organization with a forward-thinking culture.

The second reason, I suspect, is that he's a *man*. They don't tend to wrestle with this guilt the same way we working moms do.

Scott still thinks I should become an NPR correspondent. It does sound way more exciting to be writing and delivering thought-provoking, intelligent radio pieces for a national audience than it does to be writing press releases and escorting local media around a hospital.

The question is, can I have my dream job and be a great mom too? It's a lot to process.

Thank goodness for life's little escapes.

There's nothing that'll clear your head like sleeping in a damp, chilly tent with rain pouring down and two children smashed into your half-deflated twin air mattress. This week, I escaped my work-life dilemma by taking a wild one-night camping trip with my hilarious posse of church friends. (I found them at a nearby Unitarian Universalist church—an amazing place that welcomes anyone and everyone, even people like me, with murky and vague spiritual beliefs, and a conflicted history with organized religion.) It was an awful lot of work, managing this trip into the wilderness, since Ian was stuck working and I was solo mom of three. But I desperately needed to be out from under the daily grind, and to sip wine with two of my favorite women in the world, Kristina and Andrea, while our kids ran wild together in a field.

I love watching how Kristina ("Mama K" to her close friends) so calmly and effortlessly takes charge of a huge endeavor like this. With her apron on and spatula in hand, she turned a campfire grill and a couple of picnic tables covered with tablecloths into a working restaurant. I absolutely panic about arranging meals for groups. She was born to do this. Food is Kristina's escape, like singing is mine.

Between meals we helped wrangle and entertain each other's children, passed baby Daisy around the campfire, and rode a little train in wide circles around the rural campsite property until each of the nine kids got a turn at being conductor. My girlfriends' husbands, Tim and Eric, got their kicks out of "haunting" the train ride by jumping out from behind trees in the dark and terrifying the kids.

Kids picked apples, burned marshmallows, tossed footballs, hiked with flashlights and got burrs stuck in their clothes. Adults drank good wine from plastic cups, laughed, and counted our blessings—not only to have found such precious friendships, but to have one magical night together under the stars.

Lesson: When you hit a setback, soak yourself in Vitamin "F" (friendship) and Vitamin "N" (nature).

CHAPTER 21

PARENTING TRICK RIPPED FROM THE HEADLINES

September 28

It's been kind of a rough night. I'm sitting in the kitchen, freshly "denewsified," make-up off, pajamas on, trying to decompress. My insane "dinner break" routine increased in difficulty tonight. I rushed home to nurse Daisy after the 7 p.m. news and discovered Calvin had not yet done any of his homework. So there I sat, on the couch, nursing the baby, eating cold pizza and coaching Cal through math homework, while Clara stepped all over my feet and clamored for her share of attention.

Complicating matters, our 11 p.m. newscast producer had called in sick, so I was anxious to get back in the newsroom to help the other producer who had stayed late to fill in. (Cue the trite working mom quote: "If I'm at home, I feel like I should be doing more at work, if I'm at work, I feel like I should be doing more at home…")

I got Daisy fed and down to sleep, and then I tried to disappear for just one brief minute into the bathroom. Clara's screaming interrupted even that tiny sliver of solitude. "Calvin – HIT – me!! In the HEART!" She sobbed uncontrollably.

Even with our wonderful babysitter right there supervising, somehow Clara had managed to color on one of Cal's books, and he lost his temper so completely that he smacked her in the chest.

"She's a frickin' IDIOT! That's MY book! It was a GIFT!" he ranted, completely unapologetic.

I sometimes worry about his temper. He's almost 8 years old, yet he's still prone to letting his fists fly if he gets really upset. Usually, that target is Clara.

"Calvin, it's okay to be mad at her, but you *can not hit!* How do you think Clara feels?" I pressed.

"I....DON'T...CARE!!!!"

I knew it would take something dramatic to turn his mood around at this point. I grasped at straws and came up with something straight from the headlines I had just finished reading from the news desk.

"Do you know why I worry about you, Calvin?" I asked my beautiful, blond, angry boy. "I don't want you to become a bad guy. Bad guys don't care about anyone but themselves. Bad guys hurt someone when they get mad. Bad guys have bad karma. Tonight in the news, I told a story about a man who made bad choices, and hung out with the wrong friends. Do you know what happened?"

I had my son's attention.

"He got in a fight with some of those bad friends, and they shot him. He's dead." The story was tragic and true.

Cal sat listening in stunned silence. Was Mom really telling a story about guns and violence?

"And do you know his name?" I asked.

"What?" Cal wondered, his anger now totally eclipsed by intrigue.

"Calvin. His name was Calvin, just like you." This, too, was true. Reading the young man's name on the news had hit a maternal nerve.

"What did he look like?" my Calvin asked with morbid curiosity.

"He was a young man." My mind conjured up the image of the heartbreakingly young face in the mugshot. "Very handsome. I'll bet he had a mother who loved him very much," I told my son.

"I bet his mom is crying tonight," Calvin pondered.

Now we were getting somewhere.

"Yes," I said gently. "I never, *ever* want that to be us. I want you to have a good life. To make good choices. To be a good guy. To be happy and safe. Do you understand that?"

He did.

"I will always love you," I told him. "Have good dreams, okay?"

I tucked him in. I pulled out of the driveway. I went back to work.

But part of my heart stayed right there, cuddling next to my son, praying he really will stay good, and healthy, and safe.

Lesson: Some of the most powerful parenting techniques are the ones you improvise. We all feel pulled too many directions, but be proud of moments when you do the best you can with what you have.

CHAPTER 22
BILLBOARD-SIZED INSECURITY

September 29

Today I put on my red suit and got ready for my close-up. I had to pose for a billboard photo. There is something surreal seeing your own face towering over a highway, beaming down at unsuspecting drivers. One of my giant mugshots used to hang at a busy intersection near our favorite Mexican joint. "Mommy, I see you!!" Clara would yell every time we passed it. "I see you back," I'd tell her.

Today my co-worker Ericka, who anchors the 5 p.m. newscast, stood next to me in front of the makeup mirror getting ready for our photo session. We moaned together about our insecurities. "I might as well stop now," she said, as her dark, glowing skin stared back at me, absolutely flawless in the mirror. "I know I'll never be happy with how I look."

I can't see any of her flaws, if she has them, but I SO know what she means. Every woman I know thinks she has something she needs to hide. And most of us never have to see our faces somewhere as intimidating as a billboard.

People are not shy with their criticism when you're in the public eye. I've had my makeup, hair, clothing and general appearance critiqued by people calling the TV station, writing nasty comments on online forums, and even walking up to me in the grocery store. (I'm supposed to handle these situations politely, but I have always wanted to offer these people a free membership in the Get a Life Club.)

When people drive past the picture of me—the giant news anchor in the red suit, smiling down at them through perfectly penciled and glossed red lips—I wonder what they'd think if they knew the truth:

She has dried spit-up on her suit and would rather be wearing jeans.

She teased her hair four times and used half a can of hair spray to get it to cooperate.

She spackled her face with industrial-strength concealer to hide the dark blue circles beneath her eyes.

She hasn't had a solid night's sleep for more than four months since she wakes to her new baby's every grunt and rustle.

She has a love-hate relationship with the job that put her on this billboard.

She wonders if she's doing the right thing. *All the time.*

She thinks she wants too much, but can't stop wanting it.

She is not the confident, put-together, polished woman you see.

She is wandering. She is searching.

She is dreaming of something she can't yet see.

Lesson: Your inner voice is telling you the answers to your biggest questions. If you "think you want too much, but can't stop wanting it," then DO NOT STOP SEARCHING.

Truth shows up most clearly in your most fragile, insecure moments. Listen.

CHAPTER 23

A MIDWIFE'S BEST LESSON

October 1

I feel like a spoiled brat today after speaking on a panel to eager journalism students at Ball State University. From their perspectives, I have about the coolest job they can imagine. Most of them would be thrilled to get the chance to pick up some camera gear and one-man band their way around a tiny town, changing the world one story at a time.

And here I am in a major news market, on the anchor desk, in no danger (yet) of being forced to schlep my own camera gear around as a few of my colleagues are beginning to do. How dare I have the nerve to whine about the unfulfilling and overtaxing aspects of my job?

Except that *I* am living my life. They are not. Those wide-eyed students have no clue what it means to raise three children while managing a career as intense as this.

I'm remembering something that my certified nurse midwife (what a godsend!) Dana told me when I was in labor with Clara. Our home in Des Moines was only a few miles from the hospital where I planned to give birth. Dana lived nearby, and visited me at home while I was in the earlier stages of labor. "When should I go in to the hospital?" I wanted to know. I was waiting for some formula: how many minutes between contractions, or how far I was dilated.

Her advice was much less specific, but much more useful: "Stay here as long as it feels okay," she advised. "Go when you feel like you need to be somewhere else."

My first birth experience, with Calvin, had left me upset and disappointed. A very late epidural after a very long, exhausting attempt at natural labor left me too numb to push effectively. The doctor, who was filling in for the obstetrician I had grown to like and trust, was harsh and cold. Calvin's birth (via vacuum extraction that left a huge purple lump on his head) and my recovery were somewhat traumatic.

This time around, with nurturing, empowering Dana by my side for the entire labor process, things were night-and-day different.

I listened. I trusted. And indeed, I knew exactly when I hit that point where I needed to be somewhere else.

We went to the hospital at 8:30 p.m. Less than three hours later I lifted a calm and serene Clara Corinne out of the birthing pool with my own hands, smiling as I realized with awe that I had given birth completely naturally, just the way I wanted to. I had climbed my own Everest.

"Go when you feel like you need be somewhere else."

I am having that feeling once again. I can't ignore it any more than I could ignore a baby's impending birth. It's time.

It is time.

Lesson: There is no scientific formula that will tell you when change is necessary. Your instinct is the only accurate compass.

CHAPTER 24

LONG LIVE ROMANCE

October 2

I am sipping wine and fighting the old lady achiness in my bones that I always get when I am exhausted. What is that? All I want to do is climb into the hot tub and check out, only Ian hasn't filled up the darned thing, AND as usual we're all out of the chemicals needed to keep it from getting gross. So that's no good.

The house is a bit of a wreck after Clara's princess birthday party. They batted balloons around, twirled in their princess gowns, busted open a piñata, decorated princessy cupcakes, and consumed disgusting amounts of sugar. Clara made me curl her hair a little and put lipstick on her. With that stunning golden hair, the huge blue eyes, and her full, baby doll lips, she's so pretty it scares me. I can already picture her at 15, in too-short skirts and that gorgeous hair, being as clueless as I was at that age about all the impure thoughts I may have been inspiring in boys, or men. In these moments I am great with her staying five forever.

Ian's off judging a band competition somewhere near St. Louis tonight. Last night I got off work early and we had grand plans of cooking a late dinner after the kids went to sleep and making it a "date night" at home. Instead, we ate Burger King that he'd picked up on the way home from Cal's baseball practice, and went to bed early after I finished stuffing birthday party favor bags.

Still, we managed to end the night with a little…ummmm… romance. No candles and roses, but hey, I'm just glad that three kids later we still have that spark of attraction. A pretty big spark, actually. I am starting to really crave a romantic getaway—even just one night. Ian and I have such a good time together when it's just the two of us. Maybe that's because our alone time is so rare.

I think it's an encouraging sign that no matter how stressful things get at home, we never get sick of each other's company. On one Florida vacation when Cal was a baby, we were surprised by a visitor named Tropical Storm Bill, who knocked out our power.

With our baby boy asleep, we lit some candles, opened some wine and watched the sideways rain pummel the waves and our windows. It wasn't the beach vacation we were expecting. It was so much better.

Once in a while I still find myself longing for a night just like that: when we had nothing to do but love each other in the rain.

Lesson: Love is priceless and rare. Embrace stolen moments to let yourself soak in it.

CHAPTER 25
ONE THING I'M DOING RIGHT

October 3

Clara woke up today proudly announcing her new age to all who would listen. "I am 5 now!" she declared. As I write, I have just finished cleaning up the kitchen after enjoying the special dinner she requested. Ian, who loves to cook, said he would cook her *anything* she wanted, since today is her official birthday. She picked Spaghetti-O's and Velveeta Shells and Cheese. I don't think that's exactly what Ian pictured, but hey, it's not his birthday.

Our youngest has hit a different kind of milestone: a 4-month-old growth spurt. Daisy May is waking me up to nurse overnight again all of a sudden. She is a feeding machine, like the giant man-eating Audrey II plant in *Little Shop of Horrors*, begging, "Feeeed me, Seymour!!!" The dark circles under my eyes are back. Yay, parenting!

She also has a new game she plays when she's starting to get hungry. I hold her up facing me, and she makes amazing animal-like sounds as she smiles and lunges in, burrowing her head aggressively into my neck and shoulders, trying to get even closer to the food source. Then she'll lift her head, give me a gurgly smile, and start over.

Today I was heading to my favorite chair to nurse her for the umpteenth time just before leaving for work when the phone rang. It was the corporate lactation counselor provided by my TV station's parent company. I swear EVERY time this breastfeeding support staffer calls, I have my hands completely full with a nursing baby. (I think I need to check my house for hidden cameras or breast milk radar detectors.) I let the machine pick up.

The good news is that things are going pretty well for Daisy and me, in spite of my weird work schedule, so I guess I don't need the breastfeeding counseling so desperately. Still, I kind of look forward to the little cheerleading sessions. I think every working mom who is trying to nurse a baby can use a little pat on the back, and someone to say, "Hey, mama, *nice job*. You are doing backbends to make a little miracle happen for your baby, day after day after day. I know you're questioning a lot of the things you do—maybe most of them—but you are doing this thing right. Believe it, sister. You are doing just *awesome*."

Lesson: Breastfeeding a baby is a huge and important job. Make it a priority to support to nursing moms, including yourself.

CHAPTER 26

NOTHING COMPARES

October 11

What a weekend. I feel so stupid crazy lucky to have married into such a cool family. We just celebrated Canadian Thanksgiving in Indy (a first for us, I think) with Ian's mom Susan and stepdad Paul, Ian's older brother Scott, his wife Sue, and their kids Alex and Katie. Those kids walk on water in Cal and Clara's eyes.

Today after everyone had left, Calvin discovered a t-shirt that his 12-year-old cousin Alex had left behind. Cal put it on and came down the stairs. "Look, it fits me perfectly!" he said, with the shirt hanging down almost to his knees. "It smells like Alex. See?"

My heart kind of breaks because of the distance between us. Scott and Sue live in Ottawa, Ontario, which is a two-day drive or a very expensive plane trip from Indy. The cool part is that our visits to them always include a dose of cultural immersion. The border agents tend get very curious about the somewhat confusing story of how we are Americans, but nearly all of Ian's family is Canadian. (Long story, but I swear it checks out.)

One time when we were in Ottawa, Scott and Sue took us to visit the Museum of Civilization (which they pronounce "civil-lye-zation" just to be more adorably foreign.) "Are you sure they'll let Calvin in?" I asked Scott. "I mean, he still wipes his mouth on his shirt. Maybe the museum of pre-civilization would be better for us."

Ian and I wanted our kids to get a taste of Canadian culture, so we explained how Canada has TWO official languages, French and English, pointing out all the bilingual labels and signage. Later at night, Clara told me she wanted to learn more "Canadian words." I asked if she meant French words, like "merci" and "au revoir." No such luck. "No! Like, sorrey...and aboouut," she explained.

Unfortunately, we've only gotten to see our adored Canadian clan maybe once a year for the past couple of years, and before that hardly at all because Katie was going through chemotherapy for leukemia. She's so stunningly healthy and gorgeous right now it's hard to believe how much she's been through. She was only 3 years old when she got the awful diagnosis seven years ago.

One afternoon during their visit last week, I was sitting with Sue on our back deck. I asked her to help me wrap my mind around what it was like as parents to cope with Katie's cancer fight. "You just do it one day at a time, eh?" Sue explained in her matter-of-fact Canadian way. "You never plan anything because you don't know how she'll be feeling or what will be going on. Every plan you thought you had for your life is on hold."

I confessed to Sue that I felt like a huge, whiny baby by comparison, considering the most challenging times I'd been through didn't involve a life-threatening illness for my child, but things like coping with chronic work-life balance stress and helping my husband and son through emotional crises during our rough moves and transitions.

"No one's life was threatened, but still I felt like everything was falling apart and I had no idea how to keep it all together," I explained.

"But in a way, that *is* just as threatening as what we went through," Sue insisted. I listened, stunned at her empathy. "Your life as you knew it and your future as you dreamed it was in jeopardy. Your family felt threatened to the core. Everything you wanted and hoped for was at risk."

This was blowing me away. Someone I loved, who'd been through something as unthinkable as watching her child fight cancer, was telling me my own struggles weren't laughable by comparison, but actually legitimate.

"You know, Katie was telling me the other day how glad she was that she's healthy, and she's lucky that she doesn't have asthma or diabetes like some of her friends." Sue told me. "Yeah, *she's* the lucky one—she only had cancer! But in a way Katie is right. She's the lucky one. She went through two years of hell, but it's over now. She doesn't have autism, or diabetes, or asthma. She's healthy and happy." Perspective is an incredible thing, isn't it?

Katie and Clara dressed dolls, put on a dance routine, made paper flowers and collected acorns down by Fall Creek. Alex and Cal played baseball with their patient dads. Daisy laughed louder than I've ever heard her laugh when her Uncle Scott (who I'm convinced was put on this planet to show other guys how to be good dads) hoisted her into the air and gave her zerberts on that chubby belly. Paul offered me more savvy career guidance about finding the "best possible life raft off the Titanic," and made us decadent, to-die-for meals. Susan beamed as her grandchildren opened her generous birthday gifts and bonded with their cousins before her eyes.

It was magic. And now it's a memory. I hope we do it again before the kids get too old to be sleepless with excitement about seeing each other.

Lesson: There is always someone with a seemingly worse situation than yours, but your struggle matters.

CHAPTER 27

INHALING APPLES

October 15

I've had about five cups of coffee today to try to get my energy back after a busy, busy morning. Clara's school had a trip to Beasley's Orchard so I decided to put on the Super Mom cape and join them before starting my afternoon work shift.

We learned how to properly pluck an apple from a tree, and Clara and I practiced carefully twisting a gorgeous Golden Delicious off the branch.

My favorite moment was exploring the big barn they use to chill and store the apples. The frigid room was so aromatic you could almost *taste* the sweet, tempting apples.

Clara was in heaven. She has the nose of a bloodhound, which can cause trouble sometimes. I can never get away sneaking the last cookie. "Mom, I smell chocolate!" she will accuse. Public restrooms are minefields for her delicate nose. "I can't go in here, it smells **GROSS**!" she protests.

But here, surrounded by huge wooden crates full of chilled, ripe apples stacked to the ceiling, Clara's nose was her best friend.

She sniffed the tart air with her eyes closed, then, did an impromptu happy dance. "Mmmmmmm!!! Apples! I *looooove* this smell!!!"

I loved it too. But mostly, I loved being there to see the joy on my kid's face. Even though it meant I would be exhausted by the time I read the late news.

Some day when I look back at the juggling act I performed while my kids were young, I hope I will remember moments like this— when I made the most of my strange work hours to spend a morning in an orchard *inhaling apples* with my very favorite 5-year-old.

Lesson: Drink in those sublime moments when they appear. Take a mental snapshot. Take pride in the joyful experiences you create for yourself and your family.

CHAPTER 28

"EVERYTHING IS MORE BEAUTIFUL WITH TEQUILA."

October 17

I guess if we look back we'll remember this day as the day Calvin's fall baseball team won the championship. Not a bad day for the big guy—he hit a home run to help his Yankees to victory. That actually sounds better on paper. Calvin's home runs are excruciating to watch. When 7-year-olds are playing, home runs only happen for one reason: *nobody can field or catch.* Cal's amazing home run hit was really just a grounder to center field. But a series missed throws and errors followed by a terrible fumble at home plate meant that even our slow-motion base-runner could round all the bases safely.

Even more impressive than the home run was how Calvin helped make the final out to end the game and clinch the championship title. (His act of heroism was *fielding a ball and actually throwing it to first base* instead of over the fence or into the dirt.) His new trophy, which is twice as tall as any of the others, now stands proudly on the white shelf against his royal blue bedroom wall.

We took the kids out to our favorite neighborhood Mexican restaurant, *La Hacienda*, to celebrate. We've become such regulars that we have the menu memorized and know all the "meseros" by name. It's less than a mile from home, making the strong margaritas even harder to resist. On its sign, the restaurant bills itself as having "The Best Mexican Food in Town." Customers absolutely pack the place every evening, sometimes overflowing onto the patio as they wait for a colorful table to open up. It is a *scene*. But so worth it.

The kids and I try to speak only Spanish with the employees, and that has helped us form even tighter bonds with them. Thanks to my remarkable high school Spanish teacher, Mary Jo (who has since become a professional dream interpreter—how cool is that?), I have a huge soft spot for Spanish, and came very close to becoming a Spanish teacher before catching the journalism bug. Ian thinks my Spanish is sexy. And thankfully, he's more amused than jealous when the waiters in our restaurant occasionally try to turn on the Latin lover charm, knowing that my poor gringo husband has no idea what they're saying.

One of my favorite waiters, Alberto, was serving us tonight. "La bebe tiene ojos bonitos, como su mama," he told me with a flirty twinkle in his eye, knowing that my gringo husband did not understand. (The baby has beautiful eyes, just like her mother.) Why do these kinds of comments sound so charmingly sincere in Spanish? Ian and I ordered their deadly-delicious Texas style margaritas. (That's why as I write, my fingers are still just a little teensy bit numb and tingly and Ian is passed out in Clara's bed. Sucker!)

The whole restaurant looked even more amazing than usual because they just got new tables and chairs, covered in the boldest and brightest Mexican landscapes. Cactuses, smiling sunshines, and farmers working in pink, orange, red and green fields danced on every surface, all lacquered and shiny and impossibly happy.

"Everything is more beautiful with tequila," I announced, before falling apart in a fit of laughter.

One of the friendliest waitresses wanted to hold Daisy. Our little ray of sunshine was full of smiles for this caring stranger. I watched this young woman embrace my baby girl with incredible tenderness—cheek to cheek, eyes closed, drinking in a heavy dose of babyness.

I don't know if this waitress is someone's mama, or just someone who loves little ones. I don't know if her day was unusually grueling, or long, or lonely. But I do know in that brief moment, she escaped to a place of pure bliss. *Gracias, mija. (Thank you, my daughter.)*

Eventually, I guess we all got a little loud and giddy, because Calvin and I started play-fighting when he kept getting his dad's borrowed sweatshirt into the refried beans. "Cuidado, loco!" I'd tell him. "Calladito, Mama!!" he mock-scolded me, basically "shushing" me like the teachers do in his class.

I noticed a table of Latino men next to us look up in shock at this little blond, blue-eyed gringo boy, not only spitting out Spanish, but doing so with a flawless accent and grammatically perfect sassiness directed at his laughing mother.

If nothing else, I know I am doing one thing right: raising our kids to speak another language and embrace another culture.

Wait, there are two things. I'm raising kids who can LAUGH with their parents. *In two languages.*

Buenas noches. It's definitely time for bed.

Lesson: Every family should have their happy place to retreat to. When things are hard, go somewhere that makes you smile.

CHAPTER 29
ANGRY PRINCESS

November 1

I've stopped shaking but the anger is still racing through my veins. I kind of can't believe this is really happening.

There's a big election tomorrow, and as always, everyone in the newsroom is stressing out and crunching and cramming, getting prepped for big election coverage. I assumed this would be like every other election I've covered, where the two main anchors share election duties. I've done my homework on the races, and I love this stuff. Whereas some people in the news business do better with scripted stories, one of my strengths has always been live and breaking news coverage.

Then I read the fine print in the election plan. My news director assigned my new co-anchor to serve as the "main anchor" for all election coverage. My job was listed as: "Anchor desk relief, as needed." New Todd is certainly very capable, talented and experienced, but he has only been in this city for two months. Neither of us had expected him to be on the air solo for most of the evening, with me sitting on the sidelines as his reliever.

I was so stunned upon reading the assignment plan that I stepped into my news director's office to ask about it, thinking maybe there'd been an oversight or mistake. Nope. He made it clear to me that he now sees me in a secondary role. "We have two co-anchors now," he reminded me, referring to the fact that I now co-anchor the 6, 7 and 11 p.m. newscasts with Todd, while another colleague has started co-anchoring the 5 p.m. show with him. "But he is the Common Thread that runs through ALL the newscasts."

"I guess I misunderstood my role," I told him, as my mind struggled in slow motion to process what this really meant. How silly of me, to expect to be an equal partner. I'm not the "Common Thread," just one of two "co-anchors."

Just as I was getting up to leave his office, he stopped me, with a little edge his voice. "If you'd like more feedback, I can tell you I was a bit surprised during the election rehearsal yesterday," he told me. He went on to tell me he thought I came across like an "anchor princess."

I thought back and remembered my brief moment of frustration at that rehearsal. The anchors were asked to test the TV monitors in the studio, and we discovered they were *way* too small for us to be able to read the election results. I was trying my best to hold up a tiny portable screen at an angle so I could read the numbers while juggling my notecards. It was mission impossible. At one point I put down the cards and said, "This isn't going to work." No tantrum, no scene, just a sigh and that comment.

I wanted to be able to read the election returns.

I wanted to be *good*. That makes me a "princess."

What burns me more is that I have always been so determined to defy the "diva news anchor" stereotype. I go out of my way to make sure I am kind, courteous and friendly to every one of my co-workers, from the producers and stage crew workers to the person who cleans the building. I pitch in to help with all things that aren't necessarily expected of me. If I'm a "princess" because I want to SEE the election results I'm reading live on the air, I think I should just go ahead and own the role. I need to start demanding bowls of M&M's with certain colors removed, or a personal assistant to powder my nose and polish my tiara.

"Men never get called 'bossy' or 'bitchy' when they try to make sure things get done right," a former colleague of mine, Jennifer, has pointed out. She has never been afraid to be a straightforward and powerful force in the newsroom. She knows her stuff. She is a born leader. She can be warm, fun and hilarious, AND she can be assertive and direct when things need to get done. I know it hasn't been easy.

In the car on my way tonight, tears began to slide down my cheek as I realized how naïve I've always been. I really thought that if I worked my hardest and was good at my job, and good to the people around me, that would be enough. I was wrong. I am not an equal. I am *secondary*.

But I can't give up now. I am NOT a "princess." I am a professional.

I am NOT going to accept being pushed into a "backup" role I don't deserve.

I will NOT let my daughters see me get trampled on because I'm afraid to stick up for myself.

I'm ready to kick some ASS on my election night "backup" duties tomorrow. But right now, I have a baby to nurse.

Hear. Me. Roar.

Lesson: Let setbacks empower you and strengthen your resolve. Don't accept unfair or biased treatment. Speak up, seek change, or seek a better environment.

CHAPTER 30

METOL FIST (NEW BAND. THEAY ROCK.)

November 5

Yesterday began with a crisis: my boy's head was full of creepy crawly lice. "IAN!" I yelled down the stairs. "We have an emergency!"

But as I was dashing home from the drug store with the killer shampoo and teeny comb, I found out my dear friend Kristina's son Donovan is in the hospital with a bone infection. He'll spend at least six weeks on IV antibiotics. All we need is one toxic bottle of shampoo and a few piles of laundry. I feel like such a whiner.

After being de-loused, Calvin called his buddy Donovan, who is the other half of the almost-famous rock band, MetOl Fist. They've had exactly two living room rehearsals, but feel they are on their way to stardom. Their band poster is a drawing of a gray fist, with words in black marker: "MetOl Fist. New Band. Theay Rock."

MetOl Fist's songs have fantastic lyrics, including: "Baby the world is waking up, so get out of bed and scream and shout!" Ian and I warned the boys they might get mobbed by groupies. "We just need to get jetpacks so we can fly off the stage if the girls get too crazy," Cal decided.

But their chances of getting that first gig weren't looking so good now, with the lead guitarist sick in the hospital. "I heard you're in the hospital," Cal told Donovan on the phone. "Did they have to stick you with lots of needles?" Way to cheer the guy up, Cal.

Tomorrow we plan to bring some games to the hospital room and let the guys have a songwriting session. Doesn't the best art grow out of angst and trauma anyway?

MetOl Fist stops for nothing. Not even an IV. Rock on, boys.

Lesson: Sometimes the thing to do is plain and simple: "Get out of bed and scream and shout."

CHAPTER 31

FIGHT OR FLIGHT?

November 14

We just got back from a lightning quick trip home to Chicagoland to celebrate my dad's 60th birthday. The party was nice and everything, but I really think the biggest cause for celebration was Calvin FINISHING his very first long book and BRAGGING about how much smarter he feels now that he's a bona fide reader. I am still so stunned I can hardly process this.

During the entire car ride home, he had the light on, and his nose buried in the book, occasionally laughing out loud with random outbursts like, "He ATE the cheese!!!" After a while, no one even looked up.

His Nintendo DS and mini-DVD player sat untouched beside him as his eyeballs raced back and forth over the pages. "Reading is good because it makes your brain think of different things," he noted as we pulled into the driveway. "It makes you SO much smarter than TV."

I picked my jaw up off the floor quickly enough to congratulate him. Then, I congratulated myself and Ian, for adding one more thing to the list of things we're doing right: teaching a kid to love to read.

Tonight Ian is watching a disgusting zombie show. I was sitting there nursing a peaceful, sleepy baby while people on TV were literally hacking a corpse to bits and smearing zombie guts all over themselves. What would Dr. Sears say?

I eventually got drowsy Daisy down and retreated to the computer. I decided I was in the mood to take my job and shove it, so I started looking online at different open jobs. I know I want something different, but everything I see sounds either too boring or too intimidating. Pushing brand images for a pharmaceutical company? Teaching journalism to university students? That sounded good, until I saw that a Ph.D. is preferred and the woman taking applications has a background in First Amendment and copyright law. Can't I just teach them the stuff you REALLY need to know, like how to get cops to talk, how to make boring press releases sound like they belong in a newscast instead of a trash can, and how to turn a bizarre crime scene into a compelling live shot with five minutes to plan?

I've been thinking a lot about why I've been so set on leaving the TV news business. Could I live with the crazy hours if I weren't being driven crazy by management? Am I getting my brain scrambled by this fight or flight mentality?

I guess I'm starting to think I would always wonder "what if" if I opted for flight without putting up a good fight. I don't want to get chased out of the career I've spent 15 years building without taking a final stand.

So that's where I'm at tonight. Maybe I need to watch a few old westerns. When the moment arrives, I need to have the quickest draw, guns a'blazin', and my hand and head as cool and steady as a rock.

Lesson: Take a final stand before making a big life change if you feel you need to, but chances are you know in your heart when you are past the point of no return.

CHAPTER 32
THANKSGIVING FEAST: 11:30 A.M.

November 23

Today I found myself cooking two boxes of mismatched mac-n-cheese at 7 a.m. It was about midnight last night when I glanced at Clara's preschool calendar stuck to the fridge. "Thanksgiving Feast 11:30 a.m." Right. Of course. CRAP!

I probably would have known about the great Feast if I knew where to find Clara's missing backpack stuffed with important papers from school. Sadly, the backpack has fallen victim to our confusing routine of carpools and sitters.

Ian has a rehearsal all day today. I have a lunch meeting scheduled with a colleague's wife, Shelley, who is a former broadcaster-turned-corporate communications professional, said to have great perspective about leaving the news business for greener pastures. I am excited to learn what she knows. There will be no way for Clara to have her parents present at the Thanksgiving Feast.

But I didn't want to deny our 5-year-old pilgrim the chance to enjoy this school tradition. I got on the phone with my neighborhood friend and school carpool buddy Jill, who said she would be happy to help Clara through the Feast buffet, along with her little guy Matthew. "No guilt!" she warned me. "She'll do great!"

I scrounged up the only thing resembling a side dish I could think of: one box of Velveeta Shells & Cheese, one box of Kraft Macaroni & Cheese, cooking them with love and haste before sunrise and scraping them into plastic containers for the Feast.

I am thankful that at least we had name brands instead of generics to offer. It makes me feel just an ounce less incompetent as a mom. For a moment, I was almost glad I wouldn't be at the Feast in person to compare my macaroni with all the lovely homemade dishes from the more "together" parents, who I imagine have had their calendars neatly marked for the event since September.

Jill just called to check in after the Feast ended. "Clara did great," she told me. "And the kids LOVED your macaroni. It was the biggest hit at the Feast. They ate every bite."

Lesson: It's okay to be imperfect. Sometimes, it even works out better that way.

CHAPTER 33
RATTLING CHAINS

December 5

I have begun haunting Scrooge again and it feels great. For the second year in a row I am performing in "A Christmas Carol" at the big dinner theatre in town. Words cannot express how happy I am to be working in that theatre. It is my favorite escape. From the moment I walk in the scene shop entrance and smell the odd blend of sawdust, laundry soap, bleach, the buffet dinner, and hairspray, I feel like I'm where I belong.

I love chatting with the other actors as we get into our wigs and fake eyelashes and period gowns. I love the mic checks. I love hearing cast members doing their vocal warm-ups, and getting the five-minute call. I love standing backstage as the house announcements and opening music begin. I love losing myself in the scenes. I love how time does not exist when I'm on stage. I love how it feels to sing the gorgeous songs when my voice feels really strong. I love feeling an audience be moved by a moment. *Did I mention I love this stuff?*

I decided long ago to make theatre my hobby rather than my career. It wasn't an easy decision, but it was the right one. As much as I love the stage, I also love that I don't rely on it for my sole income. I am able to support my family without worrying when (or if) the next role will come. But there are certainly times I wish I could live in the theatre world much more often. I am a kid in a candy store.

This show is bringing out my more charitable and gracious side, thanks to Dickens' very obvious message. As the Ghost of Christmas Past, I guide Scrooge through the highs and lows of his life. It makes me think of the situations at work that have begun to drive me nearly insane with resentment and rage. Instead of venting angry thoughts toward individuals who have added to my stress, I picture that I am able to pluck them out of their beds in their pajamas and take them on an involuntary trip through the happier times in their life, showing them where and when they went off track.

I love to imagine that their prickly souls would warm and soften; that their inner sense of compassion and benevolence would show through.

On Friday I worked up the nerve to ask my boss if it would be possible to miss a 7 p.m. newscast in order to see Clara's school holiday program. I hesitated to even ask, because I know these requests are not usually received terribly well. And, there's the fact that I have made a formal complaint about the "princess" election coverage conversation. It's still pending formal resolution. It is super awkward at work right now, to say the least.

But my girl keeps walking around the house singing "Deck the Halls." This little show feels like a big, big deal to her. "You're coming to the show, right, Mom?" she asks regularly.

A reminder email that came from her school this week was the final straw. It read, "All the kids need is your presence. This show is their gift to you." With my stomach in a knot, I convinced myself it couldn't hurt to ask.

I got a "yes."

I know it seems a little nuts, but I can't help but think that maybe in some cosmic, karmic way, all this haunting Scrooge—on stage and in my mind—is starting to rattle the right chains.

Lesson: Allow yourself to spend time doing the things you most love. Listen to the messages those experiences stir up in your heart. Envision a more beautiful past, present and future for yourself and others.

CHAPTER 34

"OUT OF MY COLD, DEAD HANDS"

December 29

It'll be very strange tomorrow afternoon when our house is back to "normal." We've had a parade of guests visiting since the weekend before Christmas. Ian's mom, Susan, and stepdad, Paul, visited first. Clara monster-hunted with Grandma Susan, and Paul helped both kids figure out some important video game business. Susan collects dolls and LOVES to dress up her girls, so of course she gave Daisy the world's most irresistible red corduroy embroidered Christmas dress with a matching lace-trimmed bonnet. It's so cute that you can't look straight at her or your eyes will hurt.

The day after Susan and Paul left, Ian's dad, Bob, came down from Halifax, Nova Scotia. This was his second Christmas since his 20-year-marriage with Ian's stepmom ended. With Christmas traditions forever altered, we were glad to serve as a gathering place for the Shepherd siblings this year. Cal and Clara have had a great time being entertained by Ian's three younger siblings. They are the type of cool, hip, young aunts and uncles that only the luckiest kids get to have. Our kids have been baking cupcakes with thrill-seeker Auntie Meredith, building a giant snowman with quietly cool Uncle Reid and singing loud karaoke with artsy 16-year-old Aunt Elizabeth.

Christmas had plenty of highlights and only one real lowlight: Santa accidentally delivered Cal a Guitar Hero drum set for Xbox instead of for Wii. Santa must be really busy and scatterbrained.

Clara managed to talk the big guy in red into delivering yet another Baby Alive, and a set of teeny diapers. You'd think Santa would have learned from the past two years that these crying, peeing, demanding dolls are FROM HELL, but he can't seem to deny Clara the joys of plastic parenting.

Grandpa Shepherd also indulged *another* creepy doll request. This dolly can somehow stand itself up on two feet from a sitting position while babbling jibberish. If you knock it over, it cries for mama. *Loudly.* I asked about battery removal, and found out it takes several screwdrivers. (If these two Frankenbabies somehow start to collaborate, the tools WILL come out.)

My favorite memory from this Christmas trip will undoubtedly be watching 7-month-old Daisy May completely wrap up her Grandpa Shepherd in her spell. Bob hadn't yet met her, and since he was able to spend a whole week with us he's has had a chance to get to know Daisy's sweet, funny little personality. Between her deep brown eyes, her dimple, and her two-toothed grin, he was a goner. "She is just....JUST," Bob said the first day, shaking his head as he held her and stared, unable to find a word big enough.

He carries her everywhere. One little peep from her, and it's, "Oh, I think someone needs a Grandpa!" Up she goes. I've tried a few times to pry her away from him, but I got kind of a Charlton Heston feel ("...out of my cold, dead hands....") so I let it go.

I fear tomorrow will be a tough goodbye, but I am so glad that both of them got to form this bond.

Lesson: Whenever you get short and impatient with kids, remember to look at them through the eyes of a grandparent.

CHAPTER 35

MUSICAL MEDICINE

January 14

This morning Daisy May discovered a plastic toy piano. She was deliriously happy with herself— a little Stevie Wonder, feelin' the groove.

It was a pretty safe bet Ian and I would have kids with at least SOME musical inclination. Between his lifelong obsession with all things percussion and my infatuation with singing show tunes, we figured it would be tough to find any genes between us that weren't somehow infused with music. But it still amazes us to see what powerful a tool music is for all three of our kids.

When Cal gets bent out of shape we send him to the basement studio to bang on drums. He can also become hypnotized by his iPod, or Guitar Hero. Music is his pacifier.

When Clara is having a rough morning (like her mom, she's not exactly a morning person) I put on some good dance music. It's SO hard for her to hold onto a nasty mood after shaking her booty. This morning our kitchen was a wild, arm-waving tail-shaking dance party, thanks to her request: "Dynamite." Heeey-oh! Baby let...go!

Music is infallibly our best medicine. Today I decided to fight my own tendency to get all tense and stressed by prescribing a heavy dose of Sade in the car on my way to work. James Taylor is usually my go-to stressbuster. I have a theory I would like a scientist to test: that it's physically IMPOSSIBLE to be a stress case while listening to J.T. I would say the same for Sade, but there is one thing about her that stresses me out just a teeny-weeny bit: the enormous crush my husband has on her. Someone all that sultry, exotic COOLness makes me feel like a giant, boring, talentless dork. And that's not super relaxing.

Still, her CD got me through childbirth. I was a "Soldier of Love" for sure in that tub as Daisy May was being born. It turned out to be the perfect music for that incredible night. Intense and serene. Beautiful and wild. Just like my baby.

Lesson: Prescribe yourself some music therapy when you need light, comfort or strength. It's free, natural, and one of the most powerful medicines that exists.

CHAPTER 36

NO SPURS ALLOWED

February 11

The sign read: "No tank tops. No ripped jeans. No spurs." Damn, really?

What a weird world for a "news lady" to step into between evening newscasts. Ian had a country gig tonight and I used my dinner break to make a quick trip to another planet.

The place was jammed with plaid-wearing, cowboy hat-loving, cat-calling, mechanical bull-riding, tobacco-chewing, proud-to-be-a-redneck country music fans. My free-thinking church friends, Eric and Andrea, and Tim and Kristina, are always up for an adventure and met me there, along with a few other friends. "I was planning to wear assless chaps," Eric confessed. "But I got talked out of it." Tim challenged him. "Aren't all chaps assless? That's redundant, right?"

I could not resist. "Depends who's wearing them," I threw in.

Up on the stage, Ian looked and sounded great. A new friend who had joined the group asked me, "Which one is your husband?" I glanced up through the thick smoke at the stage, where the spotlights caught Ian's strong, tattooed arms as he threw down a killer drum solo. "The drummer," I said, with a schoolgirl crush grin.

I didn't even have time to say hello to him when they finished. I had to race back downtown, smelling like an ashtray. I got back on the news desk and delivered the day's news to Central Indiana.

Then, I went home to breastfeed a baby. I kissed three heads goodnight, one brown and two blonde. I added one more surreal memory to the Shepherd family scrapbook.

Lesson: Squeeze memorable experiences into the cracks of your busy life. Drink in experiences that take you outside of your comfort zone.

CHAPTER 37

CHANGE OF POWER

February 10

It's a bit uncanny that on the day a popular uprising in Egypt has helped to overthrow an aggressive dictator, a similar phenomenon seems to be happening within my news department. If rumors are correct, our news director is out.

I just got off the phone with a former co-worker, who just heard the same thing. "I feel bad for his family, and hope he is able to find a job, but he had this coming," my friend told me. "You reap what you sow."

My complaint about the princess comment and "backup relief" election night assignment was addressed in an HR meeting recently. An awkward apology resulted. It didn't help the way I felt.

But when this news began circulating, I felt the clouds hanging above my workplace crack apart, just a bit, and let a tiny ray of sun peek through. Maybe, just maybe, this change will be good. Maybe I can feel okay about going to work again.

Maybe my future will not involve moving trucks.

Lesson: Be careful not to confuse issues when you are unhappy with your situation. Some scenarios are broken on multiple levels. Filling one crack with glue can't repair a shattered vase.

CHAPTER 38
KNIFE IN THE HEART

February 16

There is always room for one more chocolate-covered strawberry. Ian carried out our Valentine's Day tradition: a homemade heart-shaped pizza and hand-dipped chocolate covered strawberries. I know diamonds are supposed to be a girl's best friend. I am so easy.

That same day, I was four minutes late to a meeting at work. I received a snide comment from the newsroom manager running the meeting ("Well, thank you for joining us, *Ms. Shepherd,*") but you know what? *I got to hand-deliver a surprise Valentine to my Clara at her class party.* You can't win them all, especially on my schedule, but Clara's face told me I had made the right call.

That's not a feeling I get very often. Today, we had temperatures above 60 degrees for the first time since November. All the horrible ice from our recent ice storm is finally starting to disappear. Clara has been bugging me for weeks to take her on a bike ride, and today seemed like the perfect day to indulge her. Right after lunch, with about a half hour to spare before I had to rush out the door to work, Super Mom loaded up the big 5-year-old in the bike buggy, climbed on and pulled the chariot a few miles around the thawing neighborhood.

Clara asked me to take her to a park. I reminded her I had to go to work. "Oh yeah," she said. "Darnit!" A few moments later, she told me, "I want to be a babysitter when I grow up." I asked her why not a news reporter like me. Her answer just about knocked me off the bike: "Because then I couldn't be with my kids very much. I would have to leave at night." Gulp. "If I'm a babysitter, even if I have to work late at night, I can be at home."

When she repeated some of this conversation to Ian later, he glanced over her head at me with eyes widened in "Oh my God" sympathy. I made the knife-twisting-in-the-heart motion. "I know..." I mouthed back to him, not wanting her to see what an emotionally charged topic this was.

Tonight, I made it home to read Clara a bedtime story and tuck her in, between anchoring three newscasts, writing two pieces for tonight's news and copyediting a huge special report.

I want her to see that somewhere between being a babysitter and being an evening news anchor, there's a perfect career for her—one that allows her to enjoy family life and professional fulfillment and won't leave her feeling torn, drained and defeated.

I hope that her search will be easier than mine; her life less conflicted.

Lesson: Don't allow yourself to be consumed by guilt when battling a conflicting situation. Power comes in understanding what you want to change in your life and searching for a new path.

CHAPTER 39

A GOOD DAY

February 25 (12:20 a.m.)

P hew! I just got home from the 11:00 p.m. news and I feel like I've just given birth again. This time, my "baby" was a three-minute special news report on serious childbirth complications linked with the drug Pitocin, often used to induce or enhance labor. It's the first time in a very long time that I've poured so much personal passion into a work project. I interviewed the doctor who led the research study, along with local doctors and women who had experienced these scary complications.

I get all geeked out about childbirth topics, mostly because I am dying to help other mothers figure out sooner what it took me three births to discover – that the status quo in American childbirth stinks. Get me going on the birth topic and it's very hard to shut me up. It's okay, and, I would argue, necessary, to ask a ton of questions, read all kinds of research and fight hard to have the kind of birth you feel best about. There are plenty of wonderful doctors, nurses and midwives out there helping women have empowered, informed and safe birth experiences, but we also have a system set up around medications and interventions that often do more harm than good. We all need to be asking more questions.

Tonight as I was pumping breast milk in the dressing room, the promo spot for my report popped onto the TV screen. There I was, lifting Daisy May out of her crib, telling moms how I was "on their side" with important childbirth information they needed to watch tonight. How strange to be sitting at work, away from my baby, watching myself holding her on the screen.

Sometimes I really beat myself up for being away from my kids so much. But tonight at least I felt that my project was worthy of that kind of sacrifice. If I'm going to be away from the three most important creatures in my life, at least I can console myself with the fact that my work may potentially have a real impact on thousands of people.

I don't want to give up journalism. But I don't want to give up on being there more for my kids. I want to know that I fought my very hardest for the best-case-scenario.

I'm pretty sure I'll find that…somehow.

Lesson: Are your "good days" so rare you can count them on one hand? If you are in a toxic situation, don't let a few ego-boosting good days confuse you.

CHAPTER 40
AMISH SPRING BREAK

March 29

Somewhere between the Double Vortex water slide, the Macarena at the kids' dance party and the lumpy hotel bed, I seem to have earned myself a triple-painkiller backache. The Aleve didn't touch it, so I'm sitting on the living room couch, waiting for some prescription meds to kick in.

I'm on spring break with the kids. While I'm not dancing on tables and getting tattooed and tanned with sand in my suitcase like a college kid, I am enjoying the break from the nightly newsroom routine. My parents invited us to an improbable tourist destination: an indoor water park in northern Indiana Amish country. Other family members came along for the adventure: my "baby" brother, Brian, his wife, Kelly (who looks WAY too good in her teeny green bikini for me to be seen next to her poolside), and their 4-year-old son, Jackson. I'll boil the weirdly wonderful trip down to a few favorite moments:

1. Amish Culture Clash

Ian and I didn't really understand what we were getting into when Mom and Dad told us about this place in Shipshewana, Ind. It is precisely in the middle of NOWHERE. We got a better idea when we passed several horse-drawn buggies on our way to the hotel. The halls and rooms were outfitted with silk floral/birdhouse themed décor and Amish mission style furniture.

"It's a DRY county," my brother Brian, the bartender/res-taurant manager, told me incredulously as we walked into the "Shipshewana suite."

I reassured him. "It's okay. We brought a LOT of beer."

A pretty young Amish girl in a white bonnet and pink dress was cleaning a room down the hall. We tried not to be gawk-ing dorks, but Kelly had to make a special trip out of the room just to make sure she got a good glimpse. After the kids were asleep, Ian, Brian, Kelly and I toasted to the cows grazing out-side our window, then gathered around our non-Amish laptop and laughed ourselves sick at stupid videos on YouTube. (For the record, the hymn "Amazing Grace" is forever ruined for me.)

2. A Grandson's Betrayal.

"Grandpa said the S-word!!" Calvin shouted, losing his mind with laughter, as he emerged from Double Vortex water slide. My poor dad, right behind him, couldn't stop laughing long enough to apologize. No apology was needed. Dad was saving my poor aching back by jumping on the grenade and taking Cal on the killer slide himself. He could've strung together every curse word in the book (and he does this with great skill, as you would know if you'd ever been around when he's working on broken appliances.) I would still have nothing but gratitude.

3. Calvin's Game Face

I loved watching Calvin pace through the arcade with his $20 free-bie game card in his hand, overwhelmed with the freedom and responsibility of choosing the right games to earn him the most tickets to buy worthless crap. He was so sad when his card ran out of money that he actually entered a HULA HOOP contest to earn an extra three bucks. When he ran out of money and tickets again, he got sulky enough to make me embarrassed. I saw my mom pull him aside to re-load his card with 10 more bucks. *Lucky stinkin' kid.* He cleaned up with an avalanche of tickets and turned them in for an awesome assortment of prizes: Chinese handcuffs; a mini whoopee cushion; a tiny deck of round cards; a ninja figurine; a plastic pirate sword; and an eye patch. SCORE.

4. Clara, Dancing Queen.

Clara hit the dance floor for the 9 p.m. kids' disco wearing nothing but a swimsuit and leaving all her self-consciousness at the door. The girl was on FIRE—hands in the air, booty shaking, turning cart-wheels, tossing her blonde hair and busting a move like it was her job.

She put the water park mascot, Buddy, to shame. As my sister-in-law Kelly put it, Buddy was as animated as a dying fish out of water. His little fish arms flopped around weakly as he shuffled in misery around the dance floor. (I could only imagine the inner dialogue of the teenager earning minimum wage for the gig.)

Clara, on the other hand, was like a happy-drunk cheerleader after four vodka Red Bulls; the life of the party.

5. Jackson's tragic loss.

My blonde mop-headed nephew with a cherub face held an im-promptu moment of silence for the tiny purple ninja figure he accidentally dropped down the elevator shaft. "Right there is where he went," Jackson told me with deep reverence as we stood inside the stopped elevator. "Right...there." He stood in the doorway staring mournfully down at that crack as though it were the open grave of a dear friend. I let him take a moment to grieve. "Are you ready now?" I asked solemnly before pushing the button.

6. Daisy going bananas.

Last night we ended up in an Amish restaurant. The food was to die for. Even little Daisy May was chowing down with her little mouth wide open like a baby bird as I shoveled in the best mashed potatoes we'd ever tasted.

There seemed to be plenty of joy to go around on our Amish splash park Spring Break adventure. I'm just hoping the pulled muscles loosen up for the second half of their plan later this week: cabin/hiking adventure at the exotic Turkey Run State Park.

Then the pie arrived. The table became very, very quiet, as we each experienced the richest, most incredible versions imaginable of our favorite pies. Dad offered Daisy a little bite of his banana crème and her eyes became giant, dark saucers. I tried to slow my father down, but if there's one thing my parents cannot resist, it's the chance to give their grandkids pure joy. The pie went into her tiny mouth so fast I still can't believe none of it came back up.

SPRING BREAK, BABY. WOO-HOO!!!!

Maybe I'm also enjoying this spring more than I normally would because of the weight that feels suddenly lifted from me. I had a promising lunch with my new general manager a few weeks ago. This week my agent had her first phone conversation with him. They talked about the news director he just hired. He has been around the Indy market for many years, and got his start at the same Illinois station I did. My agent told me that the new management team, a.): hadn't been aware of how badly my last contract negotiation went, and, b.): wants to keep me. Working out my new deal with me would be a top priority. They asked her if I was happy and if I wanted to stay.

Am I happy? Sometimes, I think, yes. But there are moments that still eat me alive. The "grass is always greener" part of me still wants to push harder for a bigger slice of the pie. I want a schedule that makes me feel like a more adequate mom. I want a paycheck that makes me feel valued and valuable. And at the end of the day, I want to feel like I've contributed something good to both my worlds, professional and personal.

It's probably too much to ask for.

But I still need to try.

Lesson: Humor is like a vitamin. Take extra doses whenever you can. Be open to different paths to your "bigger slice of the pie," but don't stop looking for that path.

CHAPTER 41

THE ACHING RETURN OF DISHRAG MAMA

April 15

"But the teacher said to wear boots that are NOT snow boots!" a tearful Clara insisted as we hurried out the door. She had a field trip day to an outdoor living history museum. Rain was possible in the forecast.

"Honey, I told you, the only boots that fit you are snow boots!" I pleaded with her. "They will have to do. I'm sure it will be fine." I negotiated as I scrambled to write a check for the field trip, find the backpack, fill the coffee mug and grab the keys. Ian is out of town at a marching band competition and this battle was mine alone. Where were the stupid snow boots, anyway?

"But she said NO SNOW BOOTS!" Clara was really starting to lose it.

I sucked in my breath. "I just…need…a moment so I don't…. get….too…angry…."

I thumped down the stairs, loaded the baby into the car, took a few more breaths, and went back to carry my still-shoeless child down the stairs with as much gentleness as I could muster.

The mini-catastrophes of daily life with kids pound my nerves so much harder when I'm short on sleep. Fridays tend to be the toughest. Five days in a row of working late nights and rising early for school leave me feeling useless and wasted. Sometimes, like last night, I even DREAM about being exhausted. I get too tired to sleep restfully. Then there are the aches. Terrible, deep aches that start in my hips and creep all the way down my legs when I am too exhausted. I haven't figured out exactly what they are, or why they happen, and neither has my doctor, but I have started calling them the "old lady aches." I know that they always seem to come when I've hit "Dishrag Mama" status—that feeling of being completely wrung dry. Advil and Tylenol can't *touch* this pain. Probably nothing could, except 12 hours of sleep not interrupted by crying babies or wailing alarm clocks.

This weekend, between baseball games, I am counting on sneaking in as many extra zzzzzz's as I possibly can, so I can have a chance of keeping my sanity the next time a crisis of snow boots proportions occurs. Please, kiddos, cooperate! Mama just needs a little rest so she can recharge the batteries.

Bye-bye, Dishrag Mama. Time to sleep.

Lesson: Your body doesn't lie when you hit your limit. When you are so chronically stressed that you have physical symptoms, it is time for dramatic and immediate change.

CHAPTER 42

VIVA, LAS VEGAS!

April 26

We did it! *Thankyouverymuch*. Ian and I are in recovery mode today after renewing our wedding vows with The King during a three-day anniversary trip to Las Vegas. We've been planning this event for much longer than we planned our real wedding 10 years ago.

I'm a lifelong Elvis nut, and I decided my obsession simply could not stop at Elvis salt and pepper shakers, paintings, purses, figurines, Christmas ornaments, or even the giant Velvet Elvis painting on the wall. My life really wouldn't have been complete without an official (and tacky) Elvis chapel wedding.

Before I would agree to marry Ian, I made him promise me that on our tenth anniversary, we'd go the *Viva Las Vegas* route and renew our vows in an Elvis chapel. Little did we know back on April 28, 2001, that by the time our Elvis ceremony rolled around we would have three children, three states, and three major career moves under our belts. We couldn't possibly have imagined back then how starved we would be for any kind of escape 10 years later, much less an escape to Sin City. Ian and I both love our children with all our life, which is exactly why we have to be on the opposite side of the country to really relax!

I tried hard not to audibly "awww..." every time we passed a child remotely close to Daisy's age during the trip. My parents graciously did the honors of manning the household while we skipped town. Just as I predicted, we returned home to find the linen closets and Tupperware shelves neatly rearranged, the laundry all washed and folded, and the grass freshly cut. (My parents are amazing. Can you hear my incredulous gulp of guilt?)

We had the perfect Vegas travel companions in our friends, Dean and Adrianna. Although Dean and Ian were college marching band buddies, I have now claimed him as my own show tunes duet partner. He is also the mayor of all things music education. "He knows EVERYBODY," Adrianna said in the airport under her breath, through the quiet grin that always seems to be on her pretty, freckled face. Sure enough, we couldn't walk five feet before Dean was spotting marching band friends or they were spotting him. Faces immediately light up when people see him. You don't just TALK with Dean. Every conversation is like a little party. I have learned never to sip my drink when he is speaking because it will inevitably wind up coming through my nose.

"This sucks, let's go home," Dean said as we basked in the desert sun outside our gorgeous hotel pool, with colorful frozen drinks in obscenely tall glasses. Dean had tried to talk Adrianna into the even LARGER-than-obscene cocktail, but as she noted quietly through her signature grin, "That wouldn't end well."

Dean and I had a cool moment floating down the lazy river, pleasantly buzzed, talking about my work situation. I told him the atmosphere is much more promising than it was six months ago. "Good!" he told me. "Because you guys can't leave."

The weekend was spent laughing, drinking, eating unbelievable food, watching mind-blowing entertainment, trying not to talk about or think about kids and stresses back home, and feeling very grateful for this opportunity to decompress.

The surreal nature of this adventure really hit me when I was standing at the back of the Elvis chapel, wearing the little ivory chiffon halter dress my girlfriend Jill K. had helped me choose. The two of us met and bonded during a children's theatre production where I played Snow White and she played my wicked step-mother. Jill plays "evil" with incredible flair, but in reality she is one of the sweetest people I know, and she has become one of my favorite partners in crime. Since Jill is also the costume designer for the theatre, she had offered to alter my dress to fit my crooked scoliosis shoulders. "You're going to look AMAZING," my sister-like friend and personal cheerleader assured me. (Yes, I'm stupid lucky to have friends like this!)

As Ian waited for me at the altar, the King himself stepped into the room. My mind raced for just a moment. "Is he on stilts?" I wondered as I stared up at him. "He's so TALL!"

I couldn't have *dreamed up* a better Elvis. The rhinestone-studded suit, aviator shades, and black sideburns were perfection. He shook his pelvis with great skill as he led us through solemn vows like "I promise to love you tender, and never return you to sender." Then, Elvis serenaded us with polished and heartfelt renditions of "Love Me Tender" and "Viva Las Vegas," asking us to link arms and sing along with him at the finale of the ceremony as we danced down the aisle.

Susan and Paul (Ian's mom and stepdad) had planned their own Vegas getaway around this momentous occasion. They watched from the pews, clapping along to the music and laughing hysterically with Dean and Adrianna. It was beautifully gaudy and unforgettable. The King stopped the ceremony for a moment to admire the Elvis ring that Ian placed on my hand.

I even got a little tear in my eye, thanks to Ian, right after the ceremony ended. "Isn't she beautiful?" Ian asked the photographer snapping photos of me standing with my cheesy bouquet.

"Aren't I lucky?" I thought to myself.

Lesson: Love and friendship deserve the royal treatment. Invest in experiences that remind you how uniquely precious your relationships are.

CHAPTER 43

PSEUDO SINGLE-PARENTING

May 1

"Are you nursing Daisy?" Clara asked from the tub the other night as I cuddled and rocked her one-year-old sister. I explained that I was done nursing, and had no milk any more. "Oh," Clara replied casually, turning back to her bath toys. "That's why your breasts are small now."

Yep. I could use a confidence boost of any kind right about now. Yesterday, I found myself being pummeled left and right by insecurity.

I had agreed to sing the National Anthem at the opening ceremony for a March of Dimes fundraising walk, not really anticipating the deep emotion that would be present. I wanted my performance to be perfect, and it was pretty far from that. I was just *barely* okay by my standards. Emotion is not a vocalist's best friend.

I was fighting back tears as I watched the hundreds of families, many of whom had lost babies to prematurity, begin stepping off on this walk. They couldn't bring back their lost children, but they could do this make a difference for other babies. Talk about hitting my soft spot. "Mamamamama," my Daisy May cooed sweet-ly from her stroller. Ian was working, as he almost always does on Saturdays, so I had the kids with me. I was so thankful this crowd was a forgiving audience.

From the march, I headed off to tackle a single-parent Saturday of baseball games, finishing a school art project, managing a homework meltdown, cooking dinner, climbing out from under a mountain of laundry, and going out for milkshakes. Thank good-ness for my friend Jeannie, a fellow baseball mom whose teeny, tiny figure makes it impossible to believe she has five children. We cheered for our little sluggers while sipping lemonade on the bleachers and catching up on hours of girl talk. Sometimes that is the best medicine.

Later at night though, once alone again, I found my fear of me-diocrity beginning to gnaw. It nagged me into second-guessing my singing ability, criticizing my post-baby body imperfections in the mirror, and worrying that my upcoming special report wouldn't be special enough to impress the new boss.

I rocked a restless Daisy who couldn't seem to stay asleep, and realized something: I am good at mothering this baby. Not just okay, not just passable, not just pretty decent. *"I'm good at this,"* I allowed myself to admit with a hint of a cocky smile. Mothering is one thing I can do well, at least lately, pretty darned consistently.

I hope I can take that little unexpected boost of confidence into the madness of this work week and USE it.

Lesson: If insecurity eating away at you, focus on your strengths. You will need confidence if you want to change your life.

CHAPTER 44

A SEAT IN THE BOYS' CLUB

May 3

Stop the presses. I just found out what it's like to have a seat in the Boys' Club.

Backing up a bit, I feel like I've been kind of on a roll lately at work with the new management, especially since I came up with a strong idea for a "May sweeps" special report when we were in dire need of good material. The topic was the shortage of women in politics in our state. The numbers are really embarrassing. I was thrilled to get the blessing to go digging into the reasons our state's leadership (like much of the country's, but even more so) is a boys' club.

As usual, when I get obsessed with a project, I've been busting my tail and working extra hours to get this report done. On top of that, the promotions team is very happy with the commercial they've just put together trying to lure viewers to watch it. "I don't have a script for this one," the promotions photographer, Steve, told me as he followed me around the Indiana statehouse.

My co-workers and I sometimes joke about Steve being the "friendly stalker." He is a sweetheart and we all love working with him. But it seems like he's always there with that camera, capturing footage that just might fit into a promo somehow. Sometimes I worry I'll turn the corner into my bathroom at home as I go to brush my teeth, and come face to face with smiling Steve and his camera, trying to catch just one last candid moment before calling it a day.

"Can you just—I don't know—talk about your story?" he asked me as we roamed the statehouse.

"Yesssss," I thought to myself. Unscripted, candid, real; this is my comfort zone. I started telling the camera about my story, just like I explained it to the curious judge in the elevator, and the state senator I just met with, and my friend Jeannie at the baseball diamond.

The promotions team finished the edit and showed the spot to the new general manager. "He had just two words," Steve told me. "Frickin' AWESOME." I'll take that.

In the midst of all this madness, we had a primary election tonight. Mostly mayoral races and city council seats were at stake. Our station assembled a team of political analysts to hash over the trends and make sense out of the numbers during our coverage. There was an attempt to bring in at least one woman, but she backed out, and we wound up with an all-male panel led by our Capitol reporter.

After the 7 p.m. newscast wrapped up, I spotted the boys' club assembled with the new news director in his office, shooting the shit and obsessively watching their phones for new numbers that were coming in rapidly. I poked my head in to say hello.

"Come on in, have a seat," my new boss invited casually. I wonder now if the shock was visible on my face.

I had a million and one things to be doing in the newsroom at that moment.

But I took that seat.

I jumped right into the political banter, picking our experts' brains, listening to their stories of what some of the major players were REALLY like, watching the right and left trade jabs and try in a rather charming way to win me over to their sides of the arguments.

The entire time, I was totally aware of how differently I was being treated compared to my experience in that very same office during last November's election. Looking around this room this time, my gender seemed not to matter in the least. I was cracking jokes with "the guys" and being treated like an intellectual equal and a leader in the election coverage. What an incredible 180 compared to six short months ago. This felt a whole hell of a lot better than being shoved into a "backup relief" role and informed of my secondary status.

"*I just got invited into the boys' club*," I marveled to myself in the car all the way home. "And I LIKED it."

Lesson: Embrace opportunities to feel powerful, and to enhance professional connections. Refuse to be intimidated by limiting gender stereotypes. Own your knowledge and ability.

CHAPTER 45

"ME-TIME" MISHAP

May 6

The day started with such promise.

Calvin's second grade project, due today, came together amazingly well in spite of our family's absence of artistic skills. We managed to get all his paraphernalia into boxes and bags, and safely off to school by 8 a.m.

It wasn't until I dropped off Clara in her classroom that I realized I was premature in giving myself a pat on the back for my parenting prowess.

Clara had left her backpack (with her lovingly-packed lunch-box inside) hanging on the banister at home, 15 minutes away. I guess I had been too preoccupied with her brother's project to double-check whether she had it.

We figured it out as I dropped her off at school. Daisy and I made a dash into a nearby supermarket to pick up Lunchables. (I know, *ick,* but she loves them and this was, after all, an EMERGENCY.) I rushed the backup lunch into her classroom.

"Oh, yes, Clara told me you forgot her lunch today," her teacher smiled at me.

Of course, "*MOM forgot my lunch*," is how my darling daughter would explain it. Not, "*I forgot my backpack.*"

I got back into the car and headed to the gym. It's been a busy, stressful week, and I felt like I deserved to do at least one tiny thing to take care of myself. I don't even really like working out, but it does feel like doing my body a favor.

A half hour was all I wanted. My cell phone rang as I pulled into the parking lot. "The story is too long," I heard the producer tell me about my special report. "We need to make some cuts. Are you ready?"

With my free minutes before work ticking away, I worked through the complicated editing over the phone, while simultaneously unloading Daisy's stroller and buckling her in, hoping to still find just enough time for a brief workout. Then, I reached for her goldfish crackers and realized the diaper bag was in the car. My car keys were in the bag. And of course the car was now LOCKED.

I ended the ill-fated phone editing session to deal with the new emergency I'd created. The lovely managers at my gym scrounged up some crackers to keep Daisy occupied while we waited for the locksmith.

The wait was 30 minutes. Just enough time. *I got that workout in.*

Then I greeted the locksmith, paid my $75, and raced my scatterbrained self home to get ready for another jam-packed day at work.

Ugh. I've got to run. My phone's blowing up again.

Lesson: Combining work and relaxation doesn't really work. Pick one at a time. It's okay to turn off your phone in order to take care of yourself.

CHAPTER 46
STEPS

May 27

I t's been a week of big steps at home.

Daisy May has started to walk. Standing in the family room she took one baby step toward me, then dropped down to those delicious little knees. I say that counts. Watching her try so hard to stay on those feet reminded me of my grandmother scolding one of my younger cousins at that age, "Don't be in a rush to start walking, baby. You'll be on those feet your *whole life*." Great advice. Why rush it?

Clara's big step involved two wheels. The other day she arrived home from school at lunchtime, and I had just 10 minutes to spare before I had to leave for work. But she *really* wanted me to help her learn how to ride that bike without training wheels.

In my high heels and "news lady" suit I raced up and down the driveway with her, keeping my hand on the back seat. Then I let go. "You've got it, *you've got it*, go - go - go - *you're doing it*!!!!" I yelled to her. Clara giggled, wide-eyed, nervous and proud. She came to a lurching stop at the end of the driveway and jumped off the bike. We were both breathless and beaming.

I got in the car and smiled all the way downtown.

Calvin had a big step of his own: trying out for the All-Star baseball team. At the tryout, I kept grabbing Ian's arm to calm my nerves. With all the coaches watching, clipboards in hand, Cal got his glove in front of a ground ball that came his way. He fired it straight to first base. I relaxed my clutch. "Oh, thank goodness," I sighed. "I know, right?" Ian smiled and squeezed my hand. We were both so proud to see our kid showing his stuff under pressure. And in the end, he got a call offering him a spot on one of the two all-star teams.

Even our nest of robins on the back porch has celebrated a big milestone. The awkward, fuzzy, bug-eyed creatures that emerged just weeks ago from delicate blue eggs have learned to fly. Ian calls them the Fab Four: John, Paul, George, and Ringo.

It's been such a week to celebrate, filled with ordinary miracles for all the little ones in our life.

May their wings take them far.

Lesson: The smallest life milestones can feel the largest. Even if they're tucked into the cracks of your frantic life, notice them and celebrate them.

CHAPTER 47
CORNFIELD WEDDING

June 12

Last night my family danced barefoot in a cornfield by moonlight. I strongly recommend this.

It was the wedding of some wonderful, artsy friends we know through Ian's music work. The bride's family lives on an Illinois farm not too far from Champaign. This turned out to be one of the most beautiful weddings I've ever experienced. The rural setting was perfect for this earthy, musical, free-spirited celebration of Larry and Lindsay, two people becoming a family.

After the vows were said, photos were taken and dinner served in a white tent next to the huge red barn, the sun began to set and the music started. One after another, groups of musicians got up on the stage set against a cornfield and played their hearts out. Calvin tossed a ball with wedding guests. Clara collected farm bugs and colored rocks. She roamed as deep as we would allow her to go into the rows of corn, and danced on a tiny wooden platform she declared her "stage."

Daisy May stood right in front of the musicians, sharing her gaping grin, pouty face, and monkey expressions with strangers.

Then she stood on those unsteady feet, threw her hands up in the air and danced like she'd been waiting all her life for this moment.

Ian got up on stage with friends and played songs I hadn't heard for many years. After dark, the chilly night breeze eventually chased us underneath quilted blankets as the music played on.

I took a mental snapshot: a silvery grain bin; a farm house and dog house; knee-high corn; a stage filled with more talented musicians than I could count; a lovely bride in a strapless, flowing ivory gown with flowers in her hair; a warm, eclectic mix of artsy guests; children becoming one with nature and music.

"I am so lucky," I thought to myself. "So happy to have married into a circle of friends where magical nights like this are possible."

I watched. I breathed. I smiled.

Lesson: Weddings are an exquisite opportunity to escape into a sacred place where time stands still and love is the main attraction. Let these occasions shine new warmth into your worn-down heart.

CHAPTER 48
FAIRY GODMOTHER

June 13

I finally had lunch with the woman everyone insists must be my long-lost sister. After spending time with her, I think she feels more like a fairy godmother.

Anne is a television journalist (once full-time, now freelance) who is revered in the community. I can see a bit of a physical resemblance between us, but I wouldn't dare compare myself to her in other ways. She's one of those exceptionally captivating people who radiates warmth, calm and a positive spiritual energy that is so strong you can *feel* her glowing. Anne's most well-known professional achievement is that she once interviewed Mother Teresa. One could easily be led to believe that some of that holiness stuck to her during that life-changing meeting, but I have a feeling Anne has had that all along.

We have bumped into each other out and about before, and exchanged friendly emails, talking about getting together sometime. Finally, obeying a strong pull, I emailed her with an invitation. "I have this feeling there is something I am supposed to learn from you. We need to get together!" I told her. I was right.

Over quesadillas and margaritas, we swapped stories about the incredible highs and lows of our journalism careers and our lives as wives and mothers. I sat riveted as she described coming to the realization that she could no longer work full-time in this career that was taking so much out of her, even though it had also added so much to her life. Anne described with profound clarity the way she felt her soul "crack open" one day when she spent hours watching a butterfly break out of its chrysalis, eventually spreading its delicate wings. I wanted to be that butterfly. I wanted to be Anne—free, grounded and spiritually centered, exactly like I dream of being, someday.

Anne also told me how she meditates every day. That has always sounded appealing to me, I confessed to her, but I could never figure out how to fit that in. "I'm talking *five minutes*," she told me. Those were magic words to me. "I sit in a sunny spot in my house facing the water, and I quiet my mind," she explained. "It has changed everything. *Everything.* Now, I could no more give up breathing or drinking water than I could give up my quiet moments."

I carried that image home with me: a sunny spot where I could breathe and be still, just for five minutes; a practice as essential as breath and air.

I found the ideal spot on our back deck—a bench in the sun. My spot. My space. For the first time in my adult life I shut the door on my life for five sacred minutes. I closed my eyes and let everything flow outward…and inward…and upward…

Lesson: When you feel a connection with someone, follow the instinct that draws you to them. Learn from their story and their energy. New friendships can awaken you to parts of yourself that have been hidden and reveal new paths worth exploring.

CHAPTER 49
WHEN TO FOLD 'EM

June 21

The summer solstice is today. It feels like summer has already been in full swing for a month. If I had time I'd make a strawberry pie and dance around a May pole just to convince myself it's official. I guess I'll have to settle for taking the kids to their first swim lesson of the season.

It's 8 a.m. and I just stepped in from sipping coffee in my Anne-inspired meditation spot on the deck, staring at the trees, and trying to figure out what to do. My agent, Sue, called yesterday. The TV station management won't budge on my request to stop anchoring the 7 p.m. newscast. They really want me back, which is good news, but they say that removing me from the 7 p.m. show would be a deal-breaker. I had it set in my mind that getting off that show would be the key to finding a slightly more do-able balance between career and family. Now, it's not an option.

I took this news pretty hard. "I shouldn't have put so many eggs in that basket," I told my agent. "But I did."

I asked myself, does one hour really make that huge of a difference anyway? Don't I always make the most of every little corner of time I have with my family? Didn't I know going into this career that it wasn't ever going to be an 8-5 job that allowed me to wave goodbye to the bus in the morning and be there for the 6 p.m. baseball game in the evening? And doesn't someone in every family have to make hard sacrifices in order to get the bills paid?

It's just that getting a break from that ill-timed newscast would have seemed like such a victory. I want so badly to prove to myself and other working parents that if you bust your tail to be valuable at work *and* have the courage to ask for what you need, you'll be able to find a reasonable arrangement that allows you to be a stellar employee AND an involved, attached parent.

One thing I have learned over the years is that you won't get anything, including a more manageable schedule, unless you ask for it. The first time I did this, at my first television job, I followed advice I had read and wrote up a proposal. I asked for a later start and end time to my schedule on just one day a week so I could have a little more time with newborn Calvin. The response I received from my childless, male manager was a definitive and unsympathetic "no." As he told me, "You knew what the job was before you had the kid."

Yes, I did know what the job was. *But I didn't know what motherhood was.* You can't know, until you're there.

I found other managers to be much more willing to accommodate scheduling requests later in my career. Again, I drew up business proposals, showing how the adjustment in hours could benefit the news operation, and explaining how invested I was in making the new schedule work seamlessly. I was so grateful for their flexibility. Even small schedule adjustments can make a night and day difference in a working parent's daily routine.

But in this case, it seems like I'm up against a wall. The burden will fall on me to make the best of an incredibly tough schedule. I'll have to keep the focus on what I *can* do, instead of what I can't.

Still, a little part of me wonders, is this the final sign that it's time to walk away and do something completely different—even though it would mean complete upheaval and financial risk?

"Remember, you don't HAVE to do anything," Ian reassured me last night. "You can walk away and we will figure it out. You have to feel good about it before you sign."

I don't feel good. But walking away right now doesn't feel like the wise thing to do. I don't want to be unemployed. (Paychecks and insurance are pretty important when you're a parent of three, right?) My back is against a wall.

And I still love journalism—some of the time, anyway. I still want the security of a contract. I think I still have it in me to do this crazy juggling act for at least a few more years in order to get us all into a more financially stable place. I *think.*

The negotiations may hit the final stage today. I am mulling over whether to make one last pitch in person for the schedule change I want, so I can at least know I went down swinging.

What am I supposed to do? What am I meant to do? What is right? What makes sense?

I am still not great at meditating, but I am spending lots of time on my bench in the sun, praying for wisdom and words.

Lesson: No matter how closely you hold your cards, negotiations are a game that you can't often win unless you are willing to walk away. You have to go in prepared to lose it all if you want to win big.

CHAPTER 50
OVER THE RAINBOW?

June 28

I signed the new contract today. All the words in the world couldn't inspire the schedule change I wanted. So I enter a new phase of my professional life with mixed feelings. I am grateful for the security and the opportunity to work in a competitive and interesting field. I am sad I have not yet been able to gain enough leverage to tilt the work-family balance into a more comfortable position.

I had a moment—a pretty convincing one—where I was on the brink of walking away from the contract. I started thinking maybe only when I am FORCED to forego the security blanket will I have the momentum to discover what might be possible in a different career.

I felt the two sides of this Alpha Mom battling. On one side, I'm the provider, angling to get the most lucrative and secure deal. On the other side, I'm the nurturer, doggedly pursuing a work scenario that leaves ample room for a normal family life. I want to do an outstanding job at something I love, bring home a nice paycheck, AND be there for "meet the teacher" nights, Tuesday night baseball games, Christmas programs and bedtime kisses. So far, I have not found the magic wand that can grant that dream. I guess it's up to me to keep searching.

It's such an ambivalent moment. I look back at how miserably lost I felt almost exactly one year ago. I can see that the situation now is a bit more promising. And I also have a ton of lingering doubt about the way I am living my life, regardless of the improvements.

I can really relate to Dorothy sometimes, spending so much time longing for that place she's heard of over the rainbow, only to realize there's no place like home. I've followed rainbows for more than a decade. I've seen Oz. Now, all I want is to click my ruby slippers and be allowed to spend more time at home. But I still keep stumbling along my winding yellow brick road.

Ian and I just poured a glass of wine and had a very ambivalent toast to "the next chapter."

Lesson: The dreams you chase aren't always compatible with the life your heart desires. Don't be afraid to click your heels when you discover a new dream.

CHAPTER 51

THE MESSAGE

July 19

The text that might change everything came while I was in the mall trying on jeans. It came from my newfound friend and "fairy godmother" Anne, the former TV journalist. I found myself exchanging messages with her as I tried to squeeze into the jeans in the tiny dressing room stall. Her messages took a sudden and intriguing turn. "My husband could use someone with your skills… if you ever wanted to get out of TV."

I texted back: Two smiley faces.

A week later, during a breakfast meeting, I nearly dropped my omelet on the floor when I heard the entire description of this job. It turns out Anne's husband is the President and CEO of Riley Children's Foundation, the fundraising arm of Indiana's main children's hospital, Riley Hospital for Children at Indiana University Health. This job would entail writing and editing a magazine, producing video pieces, and coordinating marketing communications, all with the central mission of rallying financial support for the hospital so they can give every sick child top-notch care. I decided to submit a résumé and start the application process right away.

Stories about sick or struggling children have always had a deeper pull on my heart than any other type of story. Between my own childhood journey with scoliosis, my news reporting experiences profiling an incredible set of young triplets with cerebral palsy, and my niece Katie's battle with leukemia, I feel a loud calling to do what I can to help other children going through medical challenges.

It seems hard to imagine a better combination of dream job duties than to write stories and produce videos about children who are battling health issues (unless perhaps the job also included belting out Elvis songs or show tunes, but now that's just getting greedy.)

I also know that if I were to make this career leap, there would be no more working until midnight, no more wiping away tears while checking baseball game update texts during commercial breaks on the anchor desk, and no more holidays spent in a newsroom instead of at the family dinner table.

Can I really beat the other candidates for this job and prove that a TV news anchor is ready to become a non-profit communications manager? And can I afford to take the salary hit that would come with moving into non-profit work?

I drove home with my heart pounding and my mind racing at the thought of new freedom and deeper fulfillment.

Lesson: The best opportunities often come from surprising sources. Be prepared to act fast, set your bar high and brace yourself for a leap of faith.

CHAPTER 52

FALSE EMPTY NEST

August 24

I hate, hate, HATE this schedule. I am missing everything that matters. *Everything.* Low moment. I am praying for big change.

School just began again. Clara's bus arrives at 6:57 a.m., and Calvin's a few minutes later. I got a little choked up saying goodbye to Clara on the first day. She is in full-day kindergarten now. She has never been separated from me this much. By the time she gets home from school, I'll have just started my work day. Even on slow news nights, when I can make it home on my dinner break, I will arrive home just barely in time to tuck her into bed.

My stomach hurts thinking of how little I see both of my older kids now. Thank goodness for little Daisy at home or I think my false empty nest syndrome would turn me insane.

I had to lean on my village in order to go to my second interview for the children's hospital foundation job. Ian just left town for some gigs this week so I needed help with Daisy May. "I'm looking for someone to Daisy-sit while I get interviewed," I told my friend Jeannie. "Lucky me," she replied.

While my baby charmed the pants off of my friend, I did my best to do the same to the hospital foundation people. I did some intense writing and PR campaign exercises, made my presentation, then had some time to chat with my potential future co-workers.

"This is the kind of place where we'd never keep you from attending a child's ballet recital or teacher conference," one manager assured me. "We are all about children." I nearly cried.

I am praying like mad that this works out. I decided to petition the universe today as I rode down the wooded bike path near my house. Stealing an idea from one of my favorite authors, Elizabeth Gilbert, I drafted a letter in my mind asking "the universe" for the new job to work out. I asked everyone I could think of to sign it. They all said yes. Gloria Steinem, Nelson Mandela, Elvis, Jim Henson, the Obamas, Oprah, Dr. Seuss, Dr. Sears, Governor Mitch Daniels and Maya Angelou were happy to join the cause. Friends, neighbors, former colleagues, theatre buddies, parents, siblings, cousins, church members, and all of my kids' classmates added their names.

This simply *has* to work.

Lesson: Clarity is a wonderful gift. When you really know you want something, call upon your village and the universe to support you in making it yours.

CHAPTER 53

THE OFFER

August 29

I am sitting down at the computer about to type a resignation letter to end my TV career. This is so surreal. And I'm sad to say it's taken an ugly turn.

The good news is I got a great offer for the hospital foundation job. It was a rather grueling interview process, but they chose me over the other candidates! Because the salary will be a pretty steep drop from what I've been earning in television, they are offering me a *four-day* work week, plus some flexibility to set a schedule that works well with my family. My jaw almost hit the floor.

Ian and I pored over the figures and tallied up the things we'd have to cut to make the new salary work. It will be a big change, but when you subtract the babysitting and agent fees it isn't quite as extreme as it looks. I am as excited as I have ever been, but equally terrified by the way the negotiation with my current employer is going.

When I first explained to my news director that I wanted to leave, and told him why, he seemed genuinely shocked. He told me he was expecting me to announce I was having another baby, but this news blindsided him. I listened to him second-guess my decision, explaining to me that when you're in journalism, at least you always know that your job is *interesting* as you chat with more ordinary people you meet at cocktail parties. He questioned whether, years from now, I'll be disappointed I'm only managing a "little hospital magazine" instead of anchoring the evening news. "You're a news hound," he insisted.

I appreciated his validation of my journalism skills, but not his belittling of the leap I so desperately want to make. That conversation made me realize how reluctant I have been to let my managers know what truly motivates my heart. Storytelling for the purpose of helping sick children is far more interesting and rewarding to me than almost any topic I've covered on the news. And even the most rewarding news days have become intolerable, because this schedule is INCOMPATIBLE with the family life I want.

Now, I've learned the station's management won't let me go without a fight. They say they have invested in promoting my image, and my departure will cause damage to their business.

All I can focus on right now is what is best for my kids. *I am 100% sure they need me right now more than the TV station does.* From Clara's tearful, clingy episodes that now happen several times daily, to Calvin's angry outbursts and homework struggles, it's become obvious that there is no adequate substitute for my presence in the evenings. They are suffering. I am miserable. The time has come for a huge do-over.

My stomach is in knots as I prepare to go into a meeting and find out just how difficult the management is going to make it for me to quit. I can't eat or sleep, or think about anything except for how badly I need to escape this situation that feels like a prison.

If and when it gets bad in that newsroom office today, I will hold tight to the images in my head of those three incredible little faces.

I am going to have to trust that the universe will be on our side in this conflict.

No one and nothing is going to get between this mother and her children. They are all that matters.

Lesson: When it's battle time, get strong and get ferocious. Fight for your happiness if that's what it takes.

CHAPTER 54
BATTLE

August 31

I steeled myself, resignation letter in hand, for the meeting at 2:30 p.m., only to find it had been postponed. My agent, Sue, is supposed to talk directly on the phone with the general manager instead. With the scary legal threats I've been hearing about, my nerves were so frayed, my tears so close to the surface and my stomach in such shambles that I decided I couldn't stay at work.

I left the station and cried all the way home, filled with fear and rage. How could anyone dare to stand between myself and my kids, making this huge transition even more frightening?

I arrived home to Ian's open arms and tried to pull myself together. I sat on the porch and watched first Calvin, then Clara, climbing off the yellow bus and crossing the yard toward the front door. It felt like a dress rehearsal for the new life and new schedule that was almost within reach. I nearly cracked with joy when I saw the huge smiles on their faces. A surprised Clara wanted an explanation for why I was home. "I missed you so much that I came home from work," I explained.

"Did any tears come out?" Clara wanted to know. "Yes, honey," I whispered into her golden hair as I hugged her. "They sure did."

Lesson: It's okay to take a momentary time-out from your life when you can't take any more. We all have our breaking point.

CHAPTER 55

FREE

September 2

I am 3,000 pounds lighter today. My amazing agent helped me ink a deal that lets me be FREE AT LAST! It took lots of negotiation, and it wasn't pretty, but thanks to Sue, we got it done.

I cranked up the music in my car today, opened up the sun roof and sang at the top of my lungs. "You will feel more free," I remembered Anne assuring me after I told her I was accepting the job offer and leaving television. I already feel that freedom in many ways, but that's making these last few weeks in my TV career both exhilarating and unbearable. I will miss my colleagues, but I cannot wait to say goodbye to this schedule.

I'm feeling pangs of aching sadness when I leave my kids. Somehow the separation is much harder to handle now that I see the light at the end of the tunnel. Ian has been watching me closely. "Hon, just promise me you will not beat yourself up about all that you have missed," he told me last night. "You have done a great job keeping it all together. You've been doing what you had to do." I try hard not to get lost in the guilt about all the time I have missed with them, or resentment toward the career that kept me away from them so much.

Dorothy had to trek all the way down that yellow brick road before she made it back to Kansas. This has all been part of the path to my new life.

Lesson: Resist the temptation to let regrets about the past overshadow a joyful transition in your life.

CHAPTER 56

PROST! (TO THE NEW CHAPTER)

September 18

I'm nursing a mini-hangover and slightly skinned elbow today after taking the girls up north to my brother Kevin's "Oktoberfest" party. He is the older of my two younger brothers, and he has been nicknamed "Goldenboy" for a series of reasons. Kevin was born on Christmas Day, for starters. When he went to propose to his wonderful high school sweetheart, Kim, the jeweler accidentally put a larger diamond in her engagement ring than the one Kevin had ordered. The happy couple was allowed to keep the bigger rock *at no extra charge*. Who has that kind of luck?!

My theory is that it all traces back to one memorable day when Kevin was a toddler. We were visiting my Catholic grandparents in their neat-as-a-pin brick house on Chicago's north side. Kevin walked into the kitchen holding a Virgin Mary-shaped vial of holy water that my grandmother had brought back from Lourdes, France. "Can you fill this up again, Grandma?" he asked her. "I drank it all." Thank you, Mother Mary. The kid has led a charmed life ever since.

It was no surprise that Kevin's Oktoberfest bash fell on one of those gorgeous early fall days with tons of sunshine, which poured through their newly-renovated, HGTV-worthy suburban Chicago house in the woods. "Of course it's a beautiful day," I told Kim. "It's KEVIN." Kevin is the only guy I know who could make little green caps, embroidered German shirts, polka music and bratwurst seem totally hip. Kim wore her blonde hair in little braids, and with her German heritage she looked like she belonged in a Munich biergarten. Their adorable kids, my niece Anna and nephew Zack, behaved like little angels (of course). I welcomed this chance to let loose a little, just one week before abandoning my broadcasting career and jumping into a whole new world.

The party turned a memorable corner when the adults wound up in the kids' bounce house. This one included bungee cords attached to vests, so that once enough beer was served, some of us thought it was a good idea compete to see who could make it the farthest before being snapped back by the bungee in a humiliating and painful "splat." Kim and I made quite a pair up there, bouncing forward like our lives depended on it, then suddenly being whipped backwards, braids and hair flying.

Soon, I kept thinking, I can actually participate in more of these family events without killing myself to do it. I'll have Fridays OFF. I'll get to be more of a participant in my own family and my own life.

PROST to that!

Lesson: Life transitions don't always come with ready-made rituals to commemorate them. Grab opportunities to celebrate new beginnings.

CHAPTER 57

IN THE WINGS

September 21

I got caught in the pouring rain on my bike today. It felt awesome. How often have I actually embraced the rain and let myself get totally soaked? It's my last week at the TV station and I'm feeling the need to step back, take a deep breath, and try to process everything I'm feeling.

The bike path was hypnotic. Yellow wildflowers bent under the weight of the raindrops, submitting to the rain and enjoying this cool shower that came after a hot, dry summer. I breathed in and felt really, acutely alive.

My mind flashed to campgrounds in the Big Horn Mountains of Wyoming where my family camped during my childhood. That's one of the first places I remember really having that sense of being part of a beautiful world, and being ALIVE. (The smell of pine trees and the sound of water rushing over rocks can still take me there in an instant.) Where else have I gotten that distinct feeling? My mind searched and landed on images.

Giving birth, the first, second and third time. Those magical first seconds are the most alive I can imagine feeling. But other moments flashed before me too as I rode down that rainy path: exploring new cities on trips with Ian; swimming in an icy cold lake in Sweden with my Swedish friend, Hanna; dancing and singing with friends at rock concerts; and theatre. Every theatre I have ever been a part of morphed in my mind into one archetype full of sawdust, curtains, pulleys and sandbags, mirrors and lights, shelves filled with props, sound boards and microphones, and racks of costumes. I searched my memory for the most alive part of the theatre experience, and I found it.

It's that final moment before the performance beings. Standing in the wings, smelling the dust and the lights, listening to the music begin, waiting for the curtain to rise. Once the show starts, I'm in another place, unaware of space and time. But in that moment, in the wings, everything is heightened. Something magical is about to happen. You never know exactly how it will play out.

My new life begins in a few days. But today, I'm hovering in the wings, buzzing with anticipation. The curtain is about to rise. I am so ready.

Showtime.

ACKNOWLEDGEMENTS

I owe a huge debt of gratitude to the people who helped me believe I could write for a living, the people who kept me sane during the tail end of my broadcasting career, the people who held my hand as I made the leap away from that life, and the people who encouraged me to share my story in this book.

To Ian Shepherd: Thank you for insisting that I start writing on that desperate summer day, for standing so firmly in my corner during every twist and turn, and for giving me the time and space to pursue my own dreams. I will always be grateful for your unbending love and loyalty.

To my children, Calvin, Clara and Daisy May: Thank you for giving me such *colorful* (that's a nice way to put it, right?) moments to write about, for bringing me clarity, and for hanging in there with such strength and humor as we made a big leap together. You make everything worth it.

To my wonderful parents, Del and Kathy Whitkanack: Thank you for surrounding me with love and support from day one. When you applauded my backyard musical theatre productions, sat through my television "newscasts" delivered from inside a cardboard box propped up on a piano bench, and let me use an old typewriter to create an "author's studio" in the garage, you helped me see that anything I dreamed of accomplishing was possible.

To Corinne "Corky" Sterling: Thank you for being so much more than an "auntie," and for serving as the unofficial president of all of your nieces' and nephews' fan clubs. How lucky are all of us to have you tirelessly cheering on our endeavors?

To my in-laws, Bob Shepherd, Susan Andresen and Paul Newell: Thank you for being great cheerleaders and inspiring me to reach for something better. Ian and I have found it beyond reassuring to have such a "dream team" of parents in our corner.

To my siblings and sibling-in-laws, Kevin, Brian, Kim, Kelly, Scott, Sue, Meredith, Reid and Elizabeth: I won the lottery with you guys. Each of you has made me a better person. You are great listeners and unwavering supporters for your family members. Thank you for your love, humor and loyalty.

To my "Granddad," Jim Whitkanack: Thank you for being my first and greatest teacher in the art of storytelling, for sharing your gift for poetry with me, and for always coming up with the exact words of wisdom I need to hear. I can't imagine how different my life would have been without having you to look up to, and I'm nearly certain I wouldn't have completed this book without your steady encouragement.

To Dave Shaul, John Paul and Judy Fraser: Thank you for being the perfect professional mentors, and for believing in me. You made the first chapters of my journalism career so positive and enriching, and your continued friendship and encouragement has helped me make peace with leaving that career behind.

To the leadership of Riley Children's Foundation, including Kevin O'Keefe, Vicki Mech Hester, Jason Mueller and Jim Austin: Thank you for giving me the opportunity of a lifetime, and for creating and sustaining such a flexible, family-friendly workplace culture. I count my blessings every day to have been welcomed into such an extraordinary organization.

To Maureen Manier: Thank you for teaching me so much about the craft of writing and editing for print, and for challenging me to keep taking my work to a higher level. (If only you had a nickel for every comma I deleted during editing as I imagined your sound advice!)

To Kate Burnett: Thank you for enhancing my book with your editing skills. I am grateful to have your eagle eyes involved in this project!

To David Birke: Thank you for being a great professional partner, and for helping me get the cover of the book just right. Everything I do looks a thousand times better after it passes through your hands.

To the Indy's Child and Midwest Parenting Publication family, including Barbara Wynne, Mary Cox, Wendy Cox, Susan Bryant and Karen Ring: Thank you for offering me such abundant opportunities to share stories about parenting, work-life balance, and other strange, miscellaneous topics that rattle around in my head! I am so grateful to be one small part of your impressive publishing family, and especially grateful for your support of this book.

To Sue McInerney, Napoli Management Group: Thank you for being an exceptional agent and advocate. You have been so kind and gentle with me during every step of my television career, from helping me land my "dream job," to helping me leave when I was ready. You went so far above and beyond, and I will always be grateful.

To Todd Wallace, Kevin Gregory, Ericka Flye, Terri Cope Walton, Todd Connor, John Bachman, Patrick Dix, Jennifer Tomaso, Andy Miller, and a huge list of former television colleagues who I will always admire and miss: Thank you for being wonderful partners and genuine friends. You represent the best of what broadcast journalism has to offer.

I also would like to thank the many friends and mentors who have inspired me with their own ambition and talent, helped me get this project to the finish line, taught me priceless lessons and lifted me up when I needed a boost, in particular: Anne Ryder, Mary Jo Heyen, Dana Ericson, Jennifer Kaufmann, Jolie Alois, Brooke Padilla, Mindy Manolakes, Paula Davis, Carrie Shirtz, Angela Russell, Jill Blaha, Mary Mouw, Alissa Tschetter-Siedschlaw, Hanna Forsman, Jill Kelly, Eric and Andrea Vermeulen, Tim and Kristina Riley (with special thanks to Kristina and Kellwood Photography for the cover photo), Rev. Anastassia Zinke, Jill Dempsey, Jeannie Mayhue, Cindy Hancock, Skye Davisson, Libby Turner, David Brock, Tony Mascari, Jason Rich, Scott Davis, Martha Teagle, and Dean and Adrianna Westman.

Finally, to everyone who is still struggling to leave a difficult or toxic situation, I appreciate your reading this book and listening to one more person's story. May your dreams lead you to a more peaceful, happy future.

ABOUT TRISHA SHEPHERD

 Trisha joined the nonprofit communications field after working for 15 years as a television news journalist in Illinois, Iowa and Indiana. Her reporting work earned her awards from Associated Press, Indiana Broadcasters' Association and Illinois Broadcasters' Association. Trisha is a Summa Cum Laude graduate of St. Norbert College in DePere, Wis., where she majored in Communications, Media and Theatre.

In addition to her work for Riley Children's Foundation, Trisha is an award-winning freelance writer for magazines including Indy's Child, Hamilton County Family and Cincinnati Parent, and the author of a parenting blog for IndysChild.com. Trisha, an unabashed Elvis fanatic and muscial theatre addict, lives in Indianapolis with her husband Ian Shepherd and their three children.

43086590R00085

Made in the USA
Lexington, KY
16 July 2015